T0196879

ALSO BY LYNNE SHARON SCHWARTZ

FICTION

The Writing on the Wall
Referred Pain
In the Family Way
The Fatigue Artist
Leaving Brooklyn
Disturbances in the Field
The Melting Pot and Other Subversive Stories
Acquainted with the Night
Balancing Acts
Rough Strife

NON-FICTION

Conversations with W. G. Sebald (editor)
Ruined by Reading
Face to Face
We Are Talking About Homes
A Lynne Sharon Schwartz Reader

POEMS

In Solitary

CHILDREN'S BOOKS

The Four Questions

TRANSLATIONS

Smoke Over Birkenau, by Liana Millù
A Place to Live: Selected Essays of Natalia Ginzburg
Aldabra, by Silvana Gandolfi

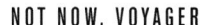

NOT NOW, VOYAGER

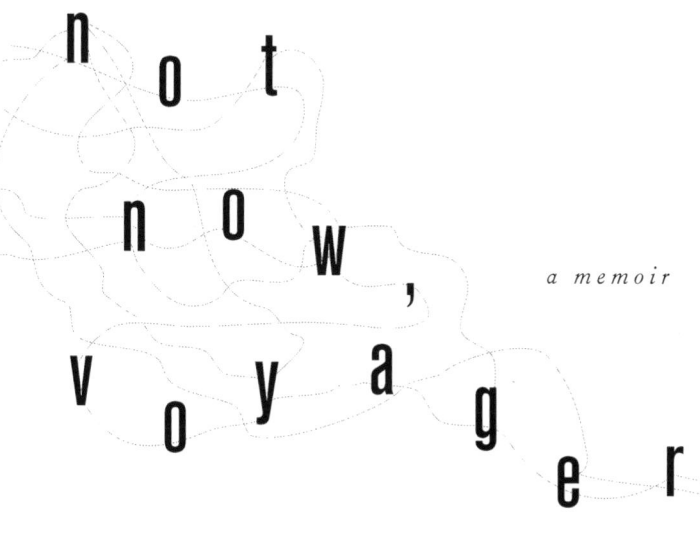

not now, voyager

a memoir

LYNNE SHARON SCHWARTZ

COUNTERPOINT
BERKELEY

Passages from this book, in slightly different form, have appeared
in *The Threepenny Review, The Southampton Review, Northwest
Review,* and *The New Orleans Review.*

Library of Congress Cataloging-in-Publication Data
Schwartz, Lynne Sharon.
  Not now, voyager / by Lynne Sharon Schwartz.
    p. cm.
  1. Schwartz, Lynne Sharon--Travel. I. Title.

G226.S38A3 2008
940.4--dc22

                                    2008050530

ISBN-13: 978-1-58243-588-6

Front cover design by Natalya Balnova
Interior design by Megan Cooney
Printed in the United States of America

COUNTERPOINT
2560 Ninth Street
Suite 318
Berkeley, CA 94710
www.counterpointpress.com

It is always a good thing to begin with renunciation, to impose a regime of abstinence on yourself from time to time. Turner lived in a cellar. Once a week he had the shutters suddenly flung open, and then what incandescence! what dazzlement! what jewels!

—HENRI MATISSE

contents

preface   xi

orkos   1

hearing roosters crow   23

borders or *cabo tormentoso*   43

clerical work   67

hotels and soap   83

no movement   111

an ugly house; speaking in tongues   131

a hand in the water   153

harmony   165

notes   173

preface

IN 2005 I COMPLETED a novel that ventured into public affairs, specifically the aftermath of the September 11, 2001 attacks. My earlier books had been more concerned with private lives, although in some sense I always thought I was writing about public affairs: the public and private permeate each other and aren't easily separated. But that last book, *The Writing on the Wall*, very explicitly moved out into the street, the city, the world. I had to read newspapers and check facts and think about large, dramatic changes in unaccustomed ways. When I was finished I felt as though I had been outdoors on a cliff for a long time, buffeted by winds, chafed and raw from exposure. I wanted to retreat to a padded room, close the door and rest from the world outside—both from living in it and writing about it. The next thing I wrote, I vowed, would be about the world inside my head; you can't get any more private than that. I wasn't sure what kind of book might result, but I wanted to try it.

But you have to write about something, after all—you can't just empty the contents of your head onto the page, tempting though that might be. To get started, you need a subject. I began thinking about traveling, perhaps because for a long time, all during the writing of that novel, I hadn't felt like stirring from home. Meanwhile all around me, friends were packing up and going off in every direction. I'd done a good deal of traveling in my adult life, protesting all the while that I didn't enjoy travel very much. Why? Not only why didn't I enjoy it, but why did I go if I didn't really want to?

As I began setting down some thoughts, what emerged was a kind of attack on travel, the idea as well as the practice. An anti-travel polemic. This might be amusing and provocative, but I soon realized it was too simple-minded. My feelings were more ambivalent. I had enjoyed traveling in the past—at least on and off; I still looked forward to new adventures. I just didn't want to move right now. Maybe not ever again, or at least not for a long time. Or, who knows, this might be nothing but a passing mood, and one day very soon I'd wake up with that unmistakable hunger for the new, the longing for the world's surprises to make *me* new.

Could I undertake a book about a passing mood? It might very well pass before the writing itself was done. So often I'd let a moment's wisp of emotion ignite a poem, or a stray conversation overheard in the street give rise to a short story. Why not indulge this odd antipathy and see where it led me?

I began exploring the ins and outs of travel—again, the idea more than the act itself. Do people really enjoy it as much as they claim? What do they truly learn in new territory? Is it something I ought to want to do, like exercise, because it's good for me?

Thinking back over my own past trips as case histories, I began jotting down a few things that remained vivid. In no sense was I writing a travel book. My notes didn't record the usual episodes one remembers from trips or reads about in travel literature. As I say in the pages that follow, I don't read travel books and wouldn't know how to write one. Travel literature is vast, I would say too vast; the last thing I wanted was to add to it. Instead, a number of strands or stories from various trips separated themselves from the fog of memory and began weaving their way through the essay. Among them were the year I spent living in Rome in 1963–64, in an odd state of superficial understanding mingled with deep-rooted ignorance, or innocence; a brief and unsettling trip I made to Jamaica in 1980, a time of acute political unrest there; and a trip to Miami Beach with an aunt and uncle when I was an adolescent, whose reverberations lasted way into the future. I realized that on these and indeed all my trips, my impressions of the moment were glib and incomplete. Later, as I thought about what I'd seen, my memories changed shape and grew more somber.

It gradually became clear that what I was writing was as much a memoir as a book exploring the idea of travel. My family began making frequent appearances; I found myself revisiting my childhood. The books I was currently reading found their way into the writing. I was enthralled by Hilary Spurling's great two-volume biography of Matisse, so I wrote about that, plus an obscure memoir about brain surgery by a Hungarian writer. Most important, I wrote about the *Tao te Ching*, which ultimately made tracks through the writing, a broad path from which some of the smaller paths diverge.

What resulted, then, did become a travel book of another sort: an illustration of the mind on a journey or quest, pausing here and there, sometimes by design, sometimes by serendipity, lingering, occasionally returning, but always on the move. In the end, I felt as if I'd managed to have my cake and eat it, a meal I've always relished. I didn't have to move physically, but I had been far afield and then circled back.

orkos

I WOKE ABRUPTLY, to a darkness so thick I could breathe it in. My mind was ominously alert, none of that blurry, dream-clogged puzzlement that usually comes with the return of consciousness. It was an alertness I often wished for in daylight—sharp, energetic, skimming through the past hours, the boat trip, the long taxi ride through flat scrubby countryside under a wide white sky, everything that had brought me here. I knew exactly where I was. I remembered the light switch on the bedside lamp even though this was a new place, my first night. I switched it on, but nothing happened. I remembered a row of square plastic buttons on the bed's headboard and fumbled around until I located them. None of them produced any light.

Now I was baffled, with panic creeping towards me like a little battalion of mice. I got up and groped my way around the room, feeling for the furniture—there wasn't much of it, as I recalled. It was pitch black and I had no idea what time it was.

Maybe it was no time at all. Maybe time had stopped and I was in the afterlife, or some place in between, a dark place, oddly enough with the same layout and furniture as my final room.

If it was not the afterlife, then it was a room in a hotel in Orkos. Orkos is a town on the Greek island of Naxos, in the Cyclades islands. I was in the middle of the Aegean Sea, on the island where Theseus abandoned Ariadne while she slept, and it was very dark. From my brief exploration shortly after I arrived, I recalled Orkos as a nowhere town, a ghost town. None of the low white buildings dotting the dry landscape had seemed inhabited. No people were on the roads. There was a beach, not quite where the guidebook had promised, in fact a good half-mile away and a trifle mangy looking, but still a beach. The hotel was pretty empty too. At dinner I'd seen four other people sitting on the dark terrace, shadowy shapes raising forks to their mouths and murmuring. The server was a vague young Norwegian who'd been sleeping when we first arrived in the sultry late afternoon. We had to seek him out in his little nook at the back and wake him.

So I was nowhere, by myself. Well, not quite. My daughter was in the room just upstairs. At least she was when I went to sleep. But if I had died in my sleep and been brought to some pitch-black limbo, I hoped she wasn't with me. She was too young; she had her life ahead of her. I would rather be dead alone than dead with her, even for company.

But of course I wasn't dead. How foolish. There had simply been some sort of electrical failure. The thing to do, in a hotel, was call the front desk and report it, ask for a flashlight. I was quite capable of that. But this kind of hotel in this kind of town didn't have phones in the room. I had a cell phone but not the kind that worked abroad. I wasn't sure why I'd brought it with me—I rarely used it even at home, but it made me feel assistance was at my fingertips. The functioning cell phone was upstairs with my daughter, along with the guidebooks. She was the organizer. On this trip, she organized and I did the talking. I was good at talking. But there was no one to talk to.

I could try going to the front desk, but that would mean finding my clothes in the dark and climbing down the series of rocky, twisting paths that led to the main building. The architecture of the hotel was unclear, diabolical, really, with the rooms laid out in clumpy outcroppings set in the hills. If there even was a front desk—I hadn't yet seen one, nor, if it existed, did this seem the kind of hotel where someone would be on duty all night. The drowsy Norwegian had led us straight from his lair to our rooms, and the dinner, lamb stew, which he proudly announced that he had cooked himself, was served on a terrace. Who could say where that terrace might be, in this hilly maze? I could go out and climb the stairs to my daughter's room in the dark, but I didn't want to wake her merely to have her share my panic, which had now crept all the way inside my head and was pattering around. Besides disturbing her, it would embarrass me. I was the mother, after all.

I tried the lights again, then sat on the bed in the dark. Where was I, not literally, but in relation to reality as I understood it? And more important, why? Where was the rest of the world with all its people? The darkness closed around me like a fleece coat. Soon it might stifle me. The night could last forever. The night was vast and I was a speck: that was the lesson of great literature and I knew it well. No one would find me in its vastness. No one would think of looking here, in Orkos. Why had I done this, left home to sit in a dark room in an endless night in a deserted town in the middle of the Aegean Sea? Ariadne was discovered and saved by Dionysus, but I had no such expectations.

I remembered a door that opened onto a tiny balcony, just large enough for one person to stand on. I groped around until I found the knob and stepped out. Light! Way up above, the moon. I almost wept with relief. It didn't light up much—there wasn't much to light up—but I could make out the silhouettes of a few sagging trees, a few right angles that must have been the rooftops of the other rooms below. There was still the moon. Perhaps there might still be the sun as well. It just might be that morning would come, and with it, light.

Nothing remained to do but lie down and wait for sleep, and for light to return. With luck, the world would not always be so dark. Never again, I vowed. If I outlive this darkness I'll never leave home again.

Orkos, the endless dark, the unknown, the isolation, the helplessness: the nightmare of travel in its purest form. Now I knew what I had always dreaded.

Ce

I know my reluctance to travel—or rather, my fretful ambivalence about it—is open to all sorts of criticism. I'm aware of the many reasons why travel is a good and desirable thing, reasons so obvious they hardly need enumerating. Today, the proliferation of ecotourism or political education tourism offers even more noble and edifying justifications. No wonder I'm slightly ashamed of my reluctance, especially as I know so many people—my husband, for one—who are forever taking flight. They live from trip to trip, in a state of eager anticipation or radiant afterglow. They come home ruddy, renewed, exhilarated, full of stories. I listen, feeling lumpy and melancholy: why didn't I go too, and have those adventures? I listen, feeling glad that I was spared all that exertion, the assault of so much novelty.

And yet I do grasp their exhilaration. I've felt it myself, in fact only a few weeks ago, on a weekend trip to Philadelphia, a time so short and a place so close to home that it barely qualifies as a trip. Sitting and daydreaming in a leafy public park on a warm early spring day with a delicious sense of freedom—nothing to do, no one expecting me—I had a vision of my daily life at home as a structure, a satisfying little architectural model. From a distance of only a couple of hundred miles, all the parts fit together organically; all the dilemmas I was embroiled in seemed manageable. Life was good. This rare contentment must be what people call perspective. It lasted a few moments, until common sense returned. Of course my life was manageable: I was too remote to have to manage it. The instant I returned home, the satisfying little model would dissolve into the usual chaos.

Weekend getaways aside, traveling is rightly considered a sign of worldliness. At its best, it shows us what is other, and we come to appreciate the grand range of otherness. At the same time we learn to relinquish the narrow view of a world divided into self and other. When I hear news reports about some place I've been, the events happening there feel more real, less abstract, rescued from the reporter's disinterested voice. I care. If there's been a natural disaster, I want to help. The people suffering are real—I've seen them on the streets and in stores and restaurants, maybe even spoken to them. If I know anyone there, I get in touch. Or if the news is happy, I'm happy too. Though news is more often of misery than happiness, while it should be the other way around: happiness is so much rarer and therefore more newsworthy. In any case, the more places I travel to, the more real the world and its people become, the more I can feel their sorrows and pleasures. By extension, if everyone traveled, we'd all become real for each other and the world would quickly become a better place, more surely than it can through the machinations of political or military leaders, whose failures make our history. Of course there are reasons—economic, ecological—that make it impractical to send hordes of ordinary citizens globetrotting, but surely it's no worse than the dismaying tactic of sending armed troops all over the place.

In a less exalted or utopian view, travel is a sign of restlessness, as well as of endurance. Whatever travel may or may not signify or accomplish, people who do it a lot are esteemed for their efforts, like people who get up at dawn to jog or practice other forms of self-discipline and mortification of the flesh. I have to believe they enjoy it as much as they claim. They certainly talk about it enough: what they saw, where they stayed, what they ate.

But I suspect there are others like me, for whom the prospect of travel, whether for business, pleasure, or pure laudable curiosity, arouses a tug of war between inertia and the pull of adventure, fear and desire. "Anxiety," Paul Goodman wrote, "is the dread of our own daring." I have good reason to dread, for my daring can be considerable, though not in the arena of travel.

On the face of it, the fear of travel is the fear of newness, of the unfamiliar. How will we manage, what will we do in strange circumstances? I once asked a friend who loves to travel—one of those people who live from trip to trip, always to farther-flung places—how he can do it with such apparent equanimity, even joy. He said his mantra at the outset is: Problems will arise, yes. And I will resolve them. I was stunned at both the simplicity and the confidence of those words. Maybe I should say that to myself every morning, I thought, to confront the new day.

Meanwhile, for those of us who don't possess such serene confidence in our coping powers, there is plenty to fear in the predicaments to be found in unfamiliar territory, but those are small daily fears. The greater fear is, Who will I be? Albert Camus rigorously endorses this fear:

> What gives value to travel is fear. It is the fact that, at a certain moment, when we are so far from our own country . . . we are seized by a vague fear, and an instinctive desire to go back to the protection of old habits. This is the most obvious benefit of travel. At that moment we are feverish but also porous, so that the slightest touch makes us quiver to the depths of our being. We come across a cascade of light, and there is eternity. This is why we should not say we travel for pleasure. There is no pleasure in traveling, and I look upon it more as an occasion for spiritual testing . . . Pleasure takes us away from ourselves in the same way that distraction, in Pascal's use of the word, takes us away from God. Travel, which is like a greater and a graver science, brings us back to ourselves.

By coincidence I saw a portion of this curiously masochistic statement emblazoned high on the wall alongside others extolling the virtues of travel, in the railroad station in Bologna, Italy, where, despite my mixed feelings, I found myself not long ago.

What a clever idea, to decorate the station walls with the thoughts of famous writers and voyagers, encouraging the febrile traveler as she drags her suitcase on its blessed wheels (to my mind, the inventor of the wheeled suitcase deserves almost as much credit as the inventor of the wheel itself) towards the savage competition that is boarding an Italian train. No doubt the selections are carefully chosen; who would want to be sent off on a journey by words such as Sinclair Lewis's in *Dodsworth*?

> It is the awful toil which is the most distressing phase of travel. If there is anything worse than the aching tedium of staring out of car windows, it is the irritation of getting tickets, packing, finding trains, lying in bouncing berths, washing without water, digging out passports, and fighting through customs.

Or in an even grimmer vein, these words from one of W. G. Sebald's disconsolate characters in *The Emigrants*:

> I cannot leave. I do not want to leave. I must not . . . Waiting at stations, the announcements on the public address, sitting in the train, the country passing by (which is still quite unknown to me), the looks of fellow passengers—all of it is torture to me.

No, those wouldn't do at all as décor for a railroad station. Even the stern Camus is preferable.

Still, the relation of travel to the self is not quite as simple or unitary as Camus supposes. Travel brings us back to ourselves, he says. But I don't feel I need to be brought back to myself. At home, at my desk writing, I'm in full possession of that self, and she wants only to stay home with pen in hand, making things up as she's done since the age of six or seven—though I didn't then foresee a future of writing. I didn't know anyone who was a writer. I couldn't conceive of someone like me, a girl from an ordinary family in Brooklyn, which I then thought the most banal of places, becoming a writer. Yet it happened.

That writing self was and is the one who feels most companionable and familiar. It's while traveling that I feel bereft. Most of me seems to have remained at home, or dormant, or in a state of suspended animation, leaving a shadow that slides unwillingly, almost mindlessly, through streets that resemble a stage set, often one excessively picturesque, such as the Sicilian beach resort masking as a simple fishing village where I spent a week, after Bologna. The setting was so picturesque—white houses set in a cliff descending to the sea, narrow streets to match, waves crashing ceaselessly against boulders—that it was almost a parody. I felt like an extra in a performance being filmed by some soon to be renowned Italian director.

Besides the charming ("charming" is a catchall word I picked up from the travel guides I've been reading) white buildings bordering the shore, the town possessed a fruit vendor with a splendid bass voice worthy of La Scala. When I first heard his arresting tones and incomprehensible syllables rising from the street, I dashed eagerly to our balcony to see what sort of crime or public demonstration was under way. But I could see nothing except the usual traffic of strolling locals and yet another band of tourists in their pastels and pendant cameras following a guide with a megaphone and an umbrella held aloft as a beacon. For several days in a row I heard the booming voice, rich and throaty, piercing, resounding through the streets and bouncing off the white buildings, more Verdi than Bellini or Donizetti, though I couldn't make out the words, which is often true of opera on the stage as well. Then one day, out on the street, I saw as well as heard him. He was driving a small truck piled with melons, figs, pears, apples, and grapes. My husband, Harry, and I rushed to catch up and bought a kilo of figs. We became part of the performance. The next day I heard him again from our window, and this time another voice joined in, a baritone, answering or arguing. They did a duet in counterpoint, a sort of Don Giovanni and Leporello routine. Whether the second voice was friend or foe, joker or rival fruit man, I never discovered.

On that recent trip to Italy I felt a sense of vacuous alienation greater than ever before. It began, or I should say its unmistakable symptom began, hours in advance of the trip itself, while I was still in native territory: it sent its warning sign, like the odd shudder that presages a flu in the offing. Harry and I had just arrived at Newark airport and unloaded our luggage; the taxi was pulling away from the curb; I was envisioning the snaking line for boarding passes, stretching out to the crack of doom. When the mini-movie in my mind got to the part where I'd show my passport, I realized I didn't have it. To be quite accurate, I thought I'd better check. In some slyer niche of consciousness, I knew. I had left it at home.

There followed a tense taxi ride back through the New Jersey wetlands towards the George Washington Bridge, during which I tried to figure out where I might have left it. Like a pulp-fiction detective, I reconstructed my moves during those last few precious moments at home. I'd finished packing and was reading a book in my usual chair in the living room, waiting for the car service. I remembered the pang in my chest when I heard the inevitable buzzer. The passport was functioning as a bookmark—I was planning to take the book to read on the plane. I leaped to my feet. Just as I had done thousands of times while reading in that chair (indeed almost every night), I reflexively—but also mischievously, or maliciously—tossed the book on the nearby coffee table and left the room.

I told the taxi driver my story and asked him to go as fast as he could, dutifully ignoring any unconscious wish to miss the plane. The driver said he didn't generally like to drive fast (most taxi drivers love to speed: why, on this particular day, did I get one who didn't?) but he would do his best. He was from Buenos Aires, but now lived in Elizabeth, New Jersey, was divorced, and had a teen-aged son, very good-looking, like his father, judging from the photograph he showed me. He also turned out to be a lover of books, so we talked about, of all things, the Argentinean writer Jorge Luis Borges. When I mentioned that I was a writer he perked up and wanted to know what I'd written, so I told him. If he got me home and back to the airport in time for my flight, I said, I would send him a book. He gave me a card with his name and address.

It was mid-afternoon and traffic was light. We got to my building in thirty-five minutes, record time from Newark. The passport was exactly where I'd expected it to be, in the middle of Colm Toibin's *The Master*, a novel based on the life of Henry James. Racing towards Newark, we discussed Borges's influence on American and European writers. We got back with time to spare; the plane was late.

Why was my dread of travel so strong, this time, that I was willing to half-consciously sabotage my trip in this most awkward and inefficient of ways? Could I foresee the degree of alienation that awaited me? Was my sense of identity growing weaker with age? It wasn't Italy itself. I've been there many times, even lived there for a year, and in some ways feel quite at home. I can even pretend fairly successfully to be Italian if I don't say more than a few words. But alienation has nothing to do with place, really; it has to do with the self, or its absence. In unpropitious conditions, the self can lose strength like a photographic negative left out too long, or lose sparkle, like soda in a bottle left uncapped. It can slowly seep away like the juice from an aging citrus fruit; all that remains is a dry light husk filled by a plangent ache.

The role of tourist, a slightly laughable one, incorporating as it does both ignorance and aimlessness, can only aggravate the weakening of identity. This time around, the sense of not belonging, of being an outsider, an intruder, was so overpowering that I began to doubt my own solidity. I had no task to do, no purpose, no reason for being there other than to see. When I was young and hadn't seen very much, seeing was purpose enough. In order to write at all, indeed in order to be a civilized person, I needed to acquire a storehouse of sights, the way a library needs to start with some basic books. Seeing is no longer enough. I need a more pressing reason for being where I am, and that reason has to do with work. With writing. My identity hasn't gotten weaker with age; my attachment to the daily life of work is stronger.

Soon after I got home weeks later, I sent the driver a copy of one of my novels but I never heard from him, maybe because it showed no traces of Borges's influence.

For other kinds of travelers, being brought back to themselves, in Camus' sense, is the last thing they want. In the nineteenth century, a number of intrepid British women set off, sometimes dressed as men and in one case as a Tibetan nun, to unearth or fashion a fresh self, to become who they were meant to be, an undertaking they found impossible in Victorian England. A 2004 show at the National Portrait Gallery in London was devoted to these women, who, according to a *New York Times* review,

> had a preference for living far from a damp, cloud-covered island where the place of women was clearly defined. Their reasons for leaving were, variously, health, curiosity, research, religion, marriage, and scandal. Their reasons for staying away were weather, power, freedom, excitement, love—and again, scandal.

Among them was Gertrude Bell, sometimes called "daughter of the desert." She learned Arabic, explored Middle Eastern archeological sites, and eventually served in British intelligence during World War I. A recent biography of Bell reveals that along with Winston Churchill, she was one of the architects, for better or worse, of the modern state of Iraq and helped write its first constitution. She could hardly be pleased by recent events there, but nor would she be as surprised, probably, or as confused as contemporary meddlers.

There was also Fanny Kemble, the nineteenth-century British Shakespearean actress who married an American plantation owner only to become horrified by the conditions she found his slaves living in. In defiance of her husband, she wrote a book exposing the evils of slavery and eventually returned to the British stage. And Anna Leonowens, known to us all from *The King and I*, a story which researchers, alas, consider more fiction than fact. After leaving the melodious children, she spent most of her later life in Canada, where she worked for women's rights and progressive education.

The most intriguing is Isabella Bird, who was born a clergyman's daughter in Yorkshire in 1831. Bird suffered from a disabling spinal ailment during her early decades in England, but when on a doctor's advice she began traveling, her symptoms vanished and she managed to climb mountains and ride elephants. After trekking around Australia, New Zealand, North Africa, the United States, Canada, Japan, China, Korea, India and Malaysia, she wrote "I still rate . . . civilization a nuisance, society a humbug, and all conventionality a crime." Evidently she wasn't troubled by what Camus warned of, an "instinctive desire to go back to the protection of old habits." *The Edinburgh Medical Journal* called Bird "The invalid at home, the Samson abroad." Besides making her a Samson, travel made Bird an influential writer: her book, *Unbeaten Tracks in Japan*, had a wide readership in that country and elsewhere.

Travel, for me, is a distraction from writing—from living— but it turned a number of these women into writers, and not the kind who advise on the most agreeable hotels and most savory restaurants. They sent dispatches from the unknown, journals charting the inner transmutations wrought by new places; they did original studies in anthropology and archeology, all the while managing to indulge in love affairs and other edifying pursuits not available to them at home.

Ordinary travelers, not the overachieving kind like Bird, will say they simply want to get away, get out of themselves for a spell—exactly the opposite of the sober trip Camus prescribes. But they're deluded. Travel can rarely be that hoped-for escape, since we haul our histories with us like carry-on baggage wherever we go. The only place we can travel without the burden of the circumstances we seek to flee is the afterlife, and no enthusiastic or reliable reports have yet come from there. Even in a presumed afterlife, chances are we can't unload our histories. We wouldn't even want to do so. After all, the salient appeal of the myth of an afterlife is that we don't have to stop being who we are.

My conflicts about travel grew entrenched when I became a writer. When I finally began doing what I had been dreaming of doing, when I got around to it. Or when it got around to me. For writing is a journey too, seeking adventure through imagination and language. You set out for unknown parts; you have a smattering of the language spoken there, and maybe you've glanced at maps or reports of similar trips by others; you have a vague idea of the places you'd like to visit, but you can't tell what they'll be like until you confront them. The only way is to go, to pick up the pen and head out. Until then it's only a fantasy, a virtual trip. The real trip turns out to be one without boundaries, endless. Whether I died early or late, I would die in the middle of my work. It is destined to be unfinished. Leaving it voluntarily, as I grew older, would feel like a kind of abandonment.

Despite all that high-sounding rhetoric, I find myself on the move, in the uncomfortable state of ambivalence, often pausing along the way to check, as it were, on who I am, like an identity check at a border crossing. The self Camus says is returned to us by travel is not the self I'm reluctant to meet up with. It's the stranger I might become who intimidates me. And she feels so close; she hovers in the shadows, waiting to spring forth. Reading about those British women who made travel a way of life, who apparently loved movement as much as I'm wary of it, I feel the insistent flicker of a kinship with them. It's as if by a swift somersault, or the flip of a toggle switch, I might become one of their plucky band. Such transformations can indeed occur abruptly and shockingly, not only in private life but in the public sphere as well. Just think of how the Berlin wall came down, or the Velvet Revolution transformed Czechoslovakia.

While I'm elsewhere, my self dormant, I wait to get home, where I can sink into my living-room chair, my feet up and rejoicing at not pacing new streets. This is the moment I look forward to from about one-third of the way into any trip, the point at which I start numbering the days until my return, counting the diminishing store of vitamin pills I doled out when I packed, watching the dirty laundry accumulate until it's a bigger pile than the clothes yet to be worn: the turning point.

Just because I'm counting laundry and vitamins, though, doesn't mean I'm not enjoying myself, after a fashion. I have—perhaps everyone has—the peculiar capacity to feel mild dread and pleasure simultaneously. Isn't that the way we go through adulthood in general, come to think of it, always with the knowledge of death awaiting us at some point, but with the day-to-day novelties distracting us, and for quite long periods, from this end? Once I get home and look at photographs of myself smiling in front of some scenic wonder or monument, the trip comes to seem pleasant, even exciting. It is amazingly enhanced by the very fact of its being over.

This double-sided emotional state—pleasure and dread—struck me with clarity in that picturesque Sicilian beach resort posing as a fishing village, when our landlord, a retired bank manager, took us out on his sailboat with some friends. After half an hour or so we were a good ways into the Mediterranean and the water was choppy. There were rumors of rain, and I was faintly seasick.

I began to long for the moment when we would turn back and the white buildings on the shore would get bigger, so big that I'd think, I could swim from here if I had to—though such exertion would hardly be necessary, as I was wearing a life jacket. Even more, I wanted to head back so that our landlord would turn the motor on again and we'd no longer be rocked by the rippling Mediterranean. But I wasn't really too seasick, far less seasick than one of the other passengers, who sat with his head over the side for the entire excursion, and besides, it was glorious out on the Mediterranean in a sailboat with a bunch of voluble Italians (except for the one throwing up) and I almost wished it would never end. As soon as we turned towards shore and the motor began rumbling, I felt enormous relief as well as glum disappointment that the adventure was nearly over.

Relief, again, is what I feel at the moment of sinking into my chair at home. Not only relief that the trip is over, but relief from the burden of guilt at not enjoying myself when so many others would be having the time of their lives. Or so I must infer from their reports when they return, and from their eager questions when I do, questions that I must either answer with enthusiasm (following the unwritten rule that anyone just back from a trip must say it was stupendous) or else be judged eccentric, a spoilsport, curmudgeonly, provincial, jaded. Yet I can't help wondering whether others really have the fantastic time I feel guilty not having.

So I sink into my chair and my "real" self welcomes me back, or I welcome it. Of course this talk of real or false selves can only be a figure of speech; the notion is a hangover from my childhood. When I was very young and couldn't wait to begin my adult life, which I anticipated as a rich brew of adventure and accomplishment, what I wanted most of all was an integrated self. I was bothered that I seemed to take on various selves depending on the circumstances and the people in my vicinity. I had one self at home and one at school, one for friends and one for family, and the "true" one who emerged only in solitude, whom I alone was privileged to know.

Even in my writing, selves would split and proliferate like cells. When I was eleven I began a novel about twin girls. It was a crime novel: a body, a hotel room. I was fascinated by hotels though I had never stayed in one. To stay in a hotel seemed the pinnacle of glamour and sophistication. Actually it still does—there's something about living without domestic arrangements that is perennially alluring and lifts one into a more heady realm.

I worked on the novel in the most dismal of realms, in school, in the seventh grade. The last class on Friday afternoon was reserved for Creative Arts. The week was almost over, so I suppose the authorities thought there was no harm in spending a smidgen of time on something as harmless as the arts—an afterthought, a dessert after the meat-and-potatoes subjects. Most of the class drew or did clay modeling but a few of us were permitted to sit at our desks and write. For forty-five minutes I would cover sheet after sheet of a yellow legal pad, flipping the sheets over in haste.

The plot turned on the girls being identical. The notion of twins, like that of hotels, was another of my secret fantasies. I never imagined I was adopted, or a changeling, as so many children do, but I did suspect I might be a twin. Many of my thoughts would unreel in dialogue, as if I were speaking to someone, a double, who would receive my words with perfect understanding. I had friends, but they knew me piecemeal: only this double could receive and thoroughly grasp everything about me. My thoughts and feelings, my doings, needed to be put into words and offered to the double for validation. Until then, they felt less than real, less than achieved. The world I moved in needed words, formulated, offered, and received, to give it the definitive stamp of reality.

So I spoke to her, my imagined twin, but it was I, not she, who contributed her half of the dialogue. This left me puzzled and uneasy. Where was she? I overheard that my mother had had several miscarriages and that one of those pregnancies was twins. It wasn't out of the question, then, that I too could be a twin and my double had died at birth. I imagined that my family had conspired to keep this secret from me, thinking it would distress me, but the uncertainty and puzzlement were even more distressing. A vanished twin would account for why I felt vaguely lonely and kept trying to talk to someone exactly like myself who would understand me effortlessly, and why she didn't answer. Later on I learned that some fetuses start out as twins but one embryo fails to develop; perhaps it emerges with the placenta or just melts away somehow. I cultivated the notion that I'd been half of such a pregnancy—this notion exonerated my family from being unduly secretive—and that it was my undeveloped, unborn double whom I kept trying to talk to. That must be why my early novel had twins as its main characters, and why one of them had to die.

I didn't finish that novel. Either the term was over, or Creative Arts was abandoned, or else I lost interest or didn't know how to proceed with the plot. From that effort, though, I grasped instinctively that writing was a place to indulge one's fantasies and try on costumes, to mask and multiply the self. Yet to be so variable in real life seemed a species of bad faith, though I would never have used that expression, bad faith, back then. When I was grown, I thought, I would arrange things so that I could be the same all the time and not have to shift selves, the way a composer shifts keys to change the mood and hue of the music. This never happened. Maybe it was an impossible wish. My life now is even more fragmented and subdivided than it was in childhood, requiring ever more selves, among them the vacuous self who travels. At least I'm no longer worried about bad faith. I'm impressed by how multifaceted human identity can be, how each of us can manage to generate new and appropriate selves on demand.

Cee

After that dreadful night in Orkos, I was brought back to myself, in a manner of speaking. When I next woke it was light. Of course. Day always comes after night. We discovered that the hotel turned off the electricity at night to save money. That morning we left Orkos. We called for a taxi and the taxi came and took us away. To Naxos City, the island's capital, a delectable town with shops, restaurants, beaches—restaurants *on* the beaches—where we did and saw all the things one travels to do and see.

None of which I will describe, since I find accounts of other people's travels painfully dull. I even find my own accounts dull, when I have to respond to the inevitable questions: Where did you go? What did you see? What did you eat? I finally understood why when I came upon Yoko Tawada's explanation in *Where Europe Begins*, a surrealized account of her moving from Japan to Germany, learning to live there and speak the language:

I once read that the soul cannot fly as fast as an airplane. Therefore one always loses one's soul on an airplane journey, and arrives at one's destination in a soulless state. Even the Trans-Siberian Railway travels more quickly than a soul can fly. The first time I came to Europe on the Trans-Siberian Railway, I lost my soul. When I boarded the train to go back, my soul was still on its way to Europe. I was unable to catch it. When I traveled to Europe once more, my soul was still making its way back to Japan. Later I flew back and forth so many times I no longer know where my soul is. In any case, this is a reason why travelers most often lack souls. And so tales of long journeys are always written without souls.

Nevertheless, travel books abound, and the travel sections of newspapers expand. Readers apparently crave vicarious travel when they are not engaged in bodily travel, and they also like finding practical suggestions for future trips. I can't make myself care what hotels people stayed in or what restaurants they ate in. What I do care about is what transforming adventures they had, real or imagined, and since such adventures are usually told best in fiction, I read fiction. *Gulliver's Travels*, to my mind, is the ideal travel book.

hearing roosters crow

I WASN'T ALWAYS so reluctant a traveler. As a child, I longed to see the world. I grew up in a family where no one—well, almost no one—went anywhere except to New York State's Catskill Mountains in the summer and once in a great while, in the winter, to Florida. Miami Beach. What I wanted was the exotic and I said so. Why can't we go somewhere exotic? I asked my parents as they loaded the car for our annual trek to the mountains, and they would laugh. Exotic! It became a word they used to tease me with, and sometimes taunt. But that never stopped my craving for the exotic or my belief that it did exist, somewhere. Ironic, for nowadays the idea of the exotic is politically incorrect. To consider any place exotic is to advertise not only one's egocentricity but provinciality. We've all learned that the Other is not really Other. And while that may be a social advance, I do regret the loss of the exotic, or rather the freedom to yearn for it and to feel awestruck on finding it.

Apart from going to the Catskills, my mother, like Camus, believed travel was perilous. Unlike Camus, she believed any peril was to be actively shunned. Travel—the unknown, the unforeseen—was not merely fraught with physical danger but was morally suspect. Home was where you were supposed to be. Anyone who wanted to leave it most likely planned to do things that would be disapproved of at home—witness Isabella Bird.

My mother projected her fears onto the rest of the world: she didn't regard them as idiosyncratic, but rather universal imperatives. If by chance her fears were not widely shared, then they ought to be. She tried to get me to adopt her fear of escalators, a minor mode of travel, or at least not to ride on them, when the only thing wrong with escalators was that they gave her vertigo. I have no problem with escalators, but it's possible that my mother's fear of travel seeped into me insidiously, and that all the traveling I've done since has been shadowed by her influence.

Her parents disembarked in New York City from Eastern Europe around the turn of the twentieth century with four children; she was the first of the next four to be born here. She was a natural storyteller and loved shaping and polishing legends—like sculptures, chiseled, reworked, stroked—about the stream of relatives arriving straight from the boat and flopping onto the living-room sofa of their brownstone, a kind of early counterculture pad, to gather strength before heading out into the labor force. Despite this history, and despite a vivid imagination of disaster, she could not imagine life in another country—imagine, that is, life proceeding abroad as it does at home, with shopping, cooking, schooling, work and all the rest, only in another language and climate. So, inevitably, she was anxious when, soon after we were married, Harry and I set off to live in Rome for a year. He had a Fulbright grant to study urban history. My mother had to take extreme measures to ease her mind.

One day our doorbell in Rome rang and we discovered two strangers, an American couple in their fifties who introduced themselves as neighbors of my parents. They were vacationing in Rome and my mother had asked them to look in on us to see how we were surviving. This was before email and cell phones; even long-distance calls were cumbersome and expensive, so I'd been writing letters home. My parents knew we had a furnished apartment but couldn't quite picture the details. So they sent this couple. We invited them in and showed them that ours was an apartment like many others. It was on the second floor of an old building in Trastevere, a working-class neighborhood that later became gentrified and arty. Our visitors could readily see that we had a front door with a lock, one large room that served as a bed-room and living room, with chairs, a table, lamps, a rug, white curtains at the large windows overlooking the cobblestoned in-tersection, and a bed in the corner covered by a bright red bed-spread, a small kitchen and a bathroom with all the requisites. The couple were congenial and a bit amused at their mission, also pleased that they had managed to locate us, and so we sat around talking for a while until they went away and eventually home, to reassure my mother that we were living in some semblance of decency.

I thought it best not to tell the visitors that we had to turn on the water heater to get hot water and that to save money we did this only every second or third day, at which time we would do everything that required hot water: bathe, wash our hair, our clothes, and the accumulated dishes. Nor did I mention the gas tanks we used for heating—if they noticed our gas tank, or *bombola*, they didn't mention it—because my mother would no doubt have worried about its leaking or exploding. It would have been hard, however, not to notice the *bombola*. It was a gray-green color, about two feet high and four or five inches in diameter, standing near the night table beside our bed with the bright red bedspread, like an elephant in the parlor. Maybe our guests were being discreet, or maybe they thought the *bombola* was an exotic European artifact and felt embarrassed not to recognize it immediately, like a reproduction of Michelangelo's *David*.

After our year in Italy we came home on a Dutch ship, the *Rotterdam*, with all our belongings plus two ancient and beloved throne-like chairs we bought in a junk shop, and our car, a red Renault Dauphine that capriciously refused to go in reverse, so we had to be careful not to get into situations that required backing up. Both sets of parents met us at the pier with lots of fanfare, especially as I came home pregnant, a condition my mother had been urging on me for some time. I got pregnant partly because my sister-in-law wrote me that she was pregnant and I have a competitive streak. I figured Harry and I would have children some day so we might as well do it then. I wasn't sure what else to do, at that point. I hadn't been successful at my attempt to write during the year in Rome. Sometimes in desperation I even thought of reviving that old mystery story about the twins and the hotel room that I'd started in the seventh grade. I didn't do that, though. All I came up with was a story about a woman who imagined various ways of killing her husband. It frightened me to think that I could harbor such a notion, and so I dropped it. Not a very professional attitude, but I was far, then, from taking myself seriously as a writer, and from accepting my lurid fantasies with the equanimity I later acquired. It might be fun to have a baby more or less at the same time as my sister-in-law, I thought, The cousins could play together and become friends. This worked out as I planned. We did have our babies within a few weeks of each other and the cousins played together and remain good friends.

Once we gathered our things from the *Rotterdam*, without backing up we drove to my parents' house for a big welcome home dinner. The atmosphere was convivial, but no one asked a single question about our year in Rome, not then or ever since. They were not curious. Or perhaps they preferred not to know.

I was fond of that red bed in our Roman apartment where our first daughter was conceived, but then again I like all beds. I am sometimes alarmed by the pleasure I take in my bed—I mean the physical object, not the pleasures associated with bed; those are not alarming. The stillness and stasis of bed are the perfect opposite of travel: inertia is what I've come to consider the default mode, existentially and electronically speaking. Bed, its utter inactivity, offers a glimpse of eternity, without the drawback of being dead.

Even more than the bed itself, I like the act of going to bed, the prospect of having nothing more to do until the next day dawns. When it does, I'm rarely thrilled to meet it. My traveler friend's mantra—Problems will arise and I will resolve them—somehow doesn't strike the right note when climbing out of a warm bed. I've met people who claim to wake with eagerness: a new day!

What fantastic adventures will it bring? This I cannot fathom. The only time I get out of bed eagerly is when I'm in the middle of writing some story; then I become the adventurous traveler, impatient to plunge into the unknown. Otherwise, I prefer watching the day drift towards its end. In the late afternoon, I start feeling mellow, and as dusk comes on, my spirits unfurl. I delay going to bed, to savor the languor of the waning day, those last woozy dregs of consciousness. In the end I have to drag myself practically by force away from my book and to my bed—those hushed midnight hours are almost too delicious to give up.

I wish I had been the one to write the faux-travel book called *Journey Around My Bedroom*. I would have been more than qualified to do so. But as with so many books one dreams of writing, it's already been done: *Voyage Autour de Ma Chambre*, by Xavier de Maistre, brother of the better known Joseph de Maistre, who wrote on a less airy topic: political theory. Although political theory might be considered more airy—at least a trip through a room involves concrete objects. *Journey Around My Bedroom* (1790) is a nearly 200-page excursion through the author's mind, as he escorts the reader on a guided tour from his bed to his favorite chair, his desk, his window. Along this restricted route his imagination wanders freely, associatively—the charm of the narrative vying with an astonishing self-indulgence—lingering on his love life, his cat, his manservant. I understand the impulse behind his book in a visceral way. Surely Xavier de Maistre felt just as I do—how much easier it is to let the mind, rather than the body, do the traveling. No tickets or schedules, no borders, no passports. Thought is the one thing that remains free no matter what changes outside the head.

Besides being an assertion of freedom, *Voyage Autour de Ma Chambre* is a piquant mockery of the notion of travel, possibly inspired by the travel literature of the time. Yet Joseph de Maistre, in the introduction to his brother's book, explicitly states that "it was not Xavier's intention to cast aspersions on the heroic deeds of the great travelers of the past." Maybe not. He might have been casting aspersions not on the travelers themselves but on their soulless reports.

(ℓ)

De Maistre must have known that too much displacement hollows out the self. Or overcrowds it, if you reach Camus' state of ideal porousness, quivering to the depths of your being at the slightest touch. Then the inner space becomes too densely seeded. There's not enough room to mull in.

> If you let yourself be blown to and fro
> you lose touch with your root.
> If you let restlessness move you,
> you lose touch with who you are.

So says the *Tao te Ching*, the ancient book of Taoist wisdom attributed to Lao-tzu, though its authorship is more legend than reliable fact. Some years ago, a dear friend and I, close since our junior high school days in Brooklyn, decided to undertake together a study of the *Tao te Ching*. I had discovered it in a pile of books my daughter—the younger one, not the one who was conceived in Rome and later accompanied me to Orkos—brought home during a Christmas break from college. As soon as I understood what it was, I was shocked that I hadn't known about it before. I knew about Zen Buddhism. How could I not, having lived through the 1960s? But that the *Tao te Ching* was an ancestor of Buddhism I did not know. So often, as a teacher, I'd been stunned by my students' ignorance. How could they have lived so long and still be unaware of what an apostrophe is for, or what the partition of India was, or what is the difference between fiction and non-fiction? Now I felt the same about my own ignorance.

The *Tao te Ching* presented a way of living that contradicted all I had ever learned. I was raised and educated to assume that everything valuable intellectually, socially, and economically was achieved after long preparation, struggle, striving, and sacrifice. The Western way. The kind of struggle that in extreme form Matisse endured, a life of consuming labor and personal turbulence, rejection and scorn, every sling and arrow imaginable to an artist. Now when his genius is unquestioned (apart from the foolish charge that his work is merely decorative), it is hard to believe the response of a Spanish critic who wrote in 1919 that the paintings "provoked a strange, unknown horror, something akin to an image of the cadaver of reason, the decomposing corpse of Intelligence." Comments such as these Matisse somehow absorbed and metamorphosed into a complex harmony uncannily like the informing spirit of the *Tao te Ching*.

Anyhow, my friend and I thought the *Tao te Ching* would be an excellent antidote to our early training, indeed to our lives, ambitious, never satisfied, always looking ahead to more struggle, like arduous mountain climbers clinging to footholds, panting, backsliding, recovering, finally reaching what appears to be a summit, only to find there's another, still higher, to reach. By the time you got there you might be too exhausted to appreciate the view. The *Tao te Ching* suggested that things might happen—interior revolutions great and small—in an instant, if one simply waited. It sounded at first like a classy variety of passivity, but it was really a quiet receptivity, a subliminal maturation. Rather than inching painfully up a mountain, life might be like sitting on a beach studying the patterns of the waves, something I'd always liked to do but never thought had any useful purpose: it would never get me anywhere. The *Tao te Ching* questioned the very idea of getting somewhere; or it proposed that you might get there simply by abiding, with no more visible effort than breathing and clicking your heels together. Effort would be required, but not the visible kind.

Arthur Waley, the British scholar of Eastern culture and translator of some of its most important texts, including the *Tao te Ching*, distinguishes between "historical" and "scriptural" translations, the former aiming to render what the book meant in its original time and place, the latter what it might mean to contemporary readers living in entirely different circumstances but freighted with the same intransigent, discontented human nature. His own translation, regarded as definitive, is of the historical variety. He unapologetically declares that he has gone for content rather than for beauty, literal accuracy rather than stylistic felicity. Perhaps because of this choice—someone had to do it—many other translators have produced their own versions, making the *Tao te Ching* one of the most frequently translated texts in the world. The ones I looked at, by Stephen Mitchell, Gia-Fu Feng and Jane English (a happy name for a translator), and the writer Ursula Le Guin, are of the scriptural variety.

In Stephen Mitchell's translation we discovered this verse:

If a country is governed wisely,
its inhabitants will be content.
They enjoy the labor of their hands
and don't waste time inventing
labor-saving machines.
Since they dearly love their homes,
they aren't interested in travel.
There may be a few wagons and boats,
but these don't go anywhere.
There may be an arsenal of weapons,
but nobody ever uses them.
People enjoy their food,
take pleasure in being with their families,
spend weekends working in their gardens,
delight in the doings of the neighborhood.
And even though the next country is so close
that people can hear its roosters crowing and its dogs barking,
they are content to die of old age
without ever having gone to see it.

Over these lines my friend and I disagreed, though cheerfully and non-aggressively, in the spirit of the text. For us, city dwellers both, their narrow vision of domestic bliss suggested a numbing primal suburbia—all it wanted was Sundays at The Home Depot. Still, I relished the implicit criticism of travel, in the sense of lust to get away. With the words "they are content to die of old age / without ever having gone to see" the country next door, Stephen Mitchell insinuates something approaching scorn for, or at least utter lack of interest in, travel, on the part of these inhabitants of what Ursula Le Guin calls a "utopia," a "vision of the golden age, the humane society." She, in contrast, renders the last few lines about the nearby country with the audibly crowing roosters and barking dogs simply as, "They'd get old and die / without ever having been there." The notion of being "content" that way—as if to say, what can you offer us that we don't already have?—is also absent from Feng and English's version: "And crowing cocks and barking dogs are heard across the way, / Yet they leave each other in peace while they grow old and die." Leaving each other in peace is different from being content. "Peace" adds a new ingredient, perhaps the notion that any foray across the border might involve aggression rather than benign curiosity.

Either way, how gratifying it was to see staying home finally given its due.

My friend countered that if there were a country so close that she could hear its dogs barking and roosters crowing, she wouldn't be able to restrain her curiosity to see what it was like. But I don't think she has ever been to Canada or Mexico, not that one can hear their dogs barking or roosters crowing from Manhattan. I'm not even sure she has been to the Bronx, which has few roosters left—unless there are some live poultry shops like the one a few blocks from my apartment, where an assortment of limp feathery creatures suggests a rural barnyard fallen on hard times.

Both the Le Guin and the Feng/English versions emphasize death and mention it early on, while Mitchell slips in the word "die" casually, near the end. Feng and English: "The people take death seriously and do not travel far." Le Guin: "Let him be mindful of death / and disinclined to long journeys." Does this mean that travel is so risky? Or that people should train their energies on waiting for death and not scatter them by distraction? The literal source, Arthur Waley's historical translation, differs significantly from these later scriptural ones: "The people would be ready to lay down their lives and lay them down again in defense of their homes, rather than emigrate." Emigrate? That is a far more serious matter than mere travel. The sentence hints at a war that might turn the people into refugees.

One could get dreamily lost in the labyrinth of translation and its near-infinite minutiae of choices. In this passage, I prefer the Mitchell version despite its muting of death, because of the faintly argumentative tone. In a terse endnote Mitchell says of the non-travelers: "Not that they are lacking in appropriate curiosity. But they have their priorities straight."

Waley dates the book at 240 BCE; others tentatively place it a couple of centuries farther back. According to Waley, Taoism arose in China from the earlier Quietists, who first used control of the breath as a means to cut through surface distractions—meaning just about everything the business of life demands—to reach a kernel of awareness, the consciousness of consciousness itself.

Scholarly commentaries go to great lengths to explain the meaning of the three words in the title. "Ching," easily disposed of, means "book." "Tao" means the way, not only the path one should follow to achieve wisdom, serenity, and mastery, but more significantly, the way things are, the way the universe works, which can be ruthless and intractable, but which becomes more bearable if one yields to its patterns and divagations rather than wriggles against them. Pages have been spent on defining "te," the most elusive. It means literally "virtue," but not in the common sense of "goodness." Its meaning is closer to the word's old sense—the particular nature of an object's or person's power and potentiality. "Te" signifies the way the Way moves through the world. The clearest definition I found is in Stephen Mitchell's introduction. He says the title might be translated as "The Book of the Way and How It Manifests Itself in the World," but he prudently chose to leave the original Chinese.

Arthur Waley says that "The *Tao te Ching* is not in intention (though anyone may treat it as such, if so he chooses) a way of life for ordinary people. It is a description of how the sage (*sheng*) through the practice of Tao acquires the power of ruling without being known to rule."

Though we were not sages or rulers over anything except our writings and our kitchens, my friend and I did so choose, but not wholeheartedly and not for very long. Our Western ways, our cluttered calendars, "the ten thousand things," as the *Tao te Ching* puts it, quickly caught up with us. Still, our reading left a significant residue, as if an unusual spice had been added to a commonplace casserole, flavoring the traditional ingredients with something new and tangy. The dish may look the same but no longer tastes quite the same. And perhaps it was not so ingenuous or presumptuous to think we might follow a path intended for sages and rulers. Other commentators—besides Mitchell, also Jacob Needleman, the scholar of philosophy and comparative religion, and Ursula Le Guin—interpret the verses addressed to warriors and masters as metaphorical. That is, we are all warriors and masters in our own lives, trying to govern the impulses, emotions, and entanglements that beset us daily, as well as to decide whether to move out into the world or withdraw—comparable to tactical military advances and retreats. Whether to venture out or remain safely at home. In a word, to travel or not to travel.

I would not choose the life described in the verse about the contented stay-at-homes; however utopian, it would probably bore me to tears. People who appear to lack "appropriate curiosity" irritate me and I would hate to be classed among them. A writer needs to be curious to see what the world has to offer. And so I am. For a person who is reluctant to move, I've been around. Regardless of the apprehension absorbed from my mother, I usually go when the opportunity arises, torn as I am between curiosity and inertia, desire and fear. Besides curiosity, there's a sense that one *ought* to take the opportunity to travel when it's offered. To refuse seems narrow-minded, stodgy, ungrateful. When so many people would leap at the chance of making this trip, it's positively boorish to refuse. Besides, some exciting, life-changing event might occur. It often does. I wouldn't want to miss it.

Musing this way, I can feel the adventurer within begin to stir. The stranger. It's well known that we all contain our opposites, the fascist lurking beneath the skin of the anarchist, the sentimentalist beneath the carapace of the cynic. Just so, if anxiety is closely linked to excitement—the dread of our own daring—I might well be harboring a daring traveler, an Isabella Bird, under my languor. In the blink of an eye, anxiety might be canceled and daring activated, unleashing the alien within, the anti-me. Such sudden flips are in keeping with the *Tao te Ching*'s idea that change works in unexpected ways, and on the large scale as well as the small. All during the cold war, for instance, received wisdom intoned that slowly, slowly, after endless anguish and sacrifice and maybe warfare, the repressive Eastern European regimes would be brought down. And then all at once they were over, so quickly that the TV cameras were barely ready. This is not to ignore the persevering efforts of dissidents, nor the persecutions and imprisonments, the thwarting and ruin of numberless lives. But meanwhile, other shifts had been going on beneath the surface, invisibly—"interior things," as Vaclav Havel put it. When the visible and dramatic events took place, they appeared less as a gradual thaw than as an iceberg collapsing. In an iceberg, too, interior things—long, slow transformations—are going on.

So an eager traveler might be, for me, one of what Italo Calvino, in his dreamlike narrative of Marco Polo's travels, *Invisible Cities*, calls "missed selves." Marco Polo encounters some of these selves in the course of traversing Kublai Khan's vast empires in order to report back on what he has seen. He comes to a new city:

> he sees someone in a square living a life or an instant that could be his; he could now be in that man's place, if he had stopped in time, long ago; or if, long ago, at a crossroads, instead of taking one road he had taken the opposite one, and after long wandering he had come to be in the place of that man in that square. By now, from that real or hypothetical past of his, he is excluded; he cannot stop; he must go on to another city, where another of his pasts awaits him, or some hint perhaps that had been a possible future of his and is now someone else's present.

Chances are that my missed selves will remain what Calvino calls "futures not achieved." I feel content listening to roosters crowing and dogs barking just across the border without having to see them for myself. I have been to Canada and Mexico. It was in Montreal that my two daughters, then twelve and fifteen, came to a startling realization. They were gazing into a shop window, side by side, when the older one said to the younger, My God, you're taller than I am. They stood back to back and Harry and I confirmed that it was true. Besides the height issue, in Montreal on a snowy afternoon we saw *Coal Miner's Daughter*, the biopic about Loretta Lynn, starring Sissy Spacek, which I liked very much and have seen twice more since then.

That is what I remember most from our family trip to Canada. I have no intention to disparage Canada as dull, as people are prone to do. Canada was no duller than anywhere else. Dullness, like safety, roots and ramifies from within, not without. I enjoyed my trip to Canada—as much as one can enjoy any family trip involving long stretches in a car—and often dream of moving there for refuge, like the draft resisters of the 1960s and '70s. I mention my blank memory rather to demonstrate how little I "get" or retain from travel.

Or rather it's not that I get so little but that what I get isn't what one is supposed to get—history, art, refreshment, new vistas—nor anything you need to travel to get, like tourists who buy something on the Via Veneto only to find the identical item in their neighborhood curio shop. What remains most vividly after a recent trip to Italy, for instance, is the family sitting directly in front of us on the plane—father, mother, and little girl with white-gold hair, about four and a half years old, whom they called Evelyn. The parents sat across the aisle from each other, an ordinary-looking thirtyish couple, the father pale and slender, in jeans, the mother blonde, though not so blonde as Evelyn, with her hair pulled back tight in a ponytail. On her father's lap, Evelyn screamed incessantly, short, high-pitched, animal-like shrieks. Neither parent did anything to try to alleviate her shrieking. My adrenaline surged as I remembered all the ways to distract crying children—countless ways, and one gets skilled at it, especially in public places where embarrassment is a powerful incentive. But Evelyn's parents simply sat, as if they didn't know her. I even thought of suggesting a book or a game or a song, but of course this was none of my business; and then I thought maybe there was something seriously wrong with Evelyn, autism or something of the sort (though that usually afflicts boys, not girls), and her parents knew best how to deal with her. I thought that but didn't really believe it. After a while the mother reached across the aisle and wordlessly handed her something. I peered over the seat to see. A toy fishing rod. What on earth could a child do with a toy fishing rod on an airplane except wave it around and poke someone's eye, maybe even her own.

Despite the fishing rod Evelyn kept shrieking as her parents sat like stone, until at last the shrieks grew less piercing, then subsided altogether. The father handed her across the aisle to the mother, who said in a low but stern voice, "That was unacceptable behavior." My stomach turned over and I had a small epiphany. I had witnessed everything that was wrong with contemporary childrearing, not to mention contemporary colloquial English. But my epiphany wasn't genuine. All I had seen was that there are mad people among us, looking ordinary, who methodically destroy their children, who knows out of what resentment or ignorance or delusions. But that was nothing new. I had known it before, and for a long time.

Otherwise, my travel experiences get stowed away in some attic in the mansion of the self, tossed upstairs as soon as I arrive gratefully at home. Now and then I open the door and am amazed at the wonders I find, the treasures in the attic, but I rarely move those wonders to the main part of the house.

So my curiosity about a country just across the border might be satisfied by reading books about it, or seeing films, or hearing its music or learning its language, all of which I might well do, and would consider time better spent than waiting in line at an airport security checkpoint with my shoes in my hand and my keys lying disconsolate in a plastic bin.

Lately I recalled that I am not alone. The Duc des Esseintes, the reclusive aesthete of J. K. Huysman's 1884 novel, *A Rebours*, felt the same. I had read *A Rebours* in college but forgotten all about it, except for the strain of reading it in French, weighty as it is with protracted descriptions of des Esseintes' every minute sensation. Late into the night, I would sit on the hard bed in my little eleven-dollar-a-week room in a women's residence, looking up arcane words in my French–English dictionary. The hypersensitive Duke sets off for London, and while waiting for the train in the Paris station, visits an English bookstore, stops in an English bar, and then an English tavern where he eats a typical English meal. By the end he decides he's had his London experience without all the discomforts of actual travel, though in his day there were no airplanes and no need to take off his shoes.

I would venture that a rooster is a rooster wherever it is. *Coal Miner's Daughter*, with its Appalachian setting, had a whiff of the exotic when I saw it in Montreal, but it was nearly as exotic when I saw it again in New York City. I am coming dangerously, and unwillingly, close to echoing the notorious words of Spiro Agnew, vice-president under Richard Nixon but forced to resign because of shady financial dealings and soon forgotten in the light of far worse offenses on the part of that administration. "If you've seen one ghetto you've seen them all," Agnew said, when asked if he'd visited the decaying South Bronx—offensive words he should never have uttered. But they were offensive not for what they implied about ghettos—or about any neighborhood, rich or poor—which are alike in some ways and distinctive in others. His words were offensive because a public servant's job is to be where the people are, to be physically present. I suppose one could argue, by extension, that we ought to show up in the world, be citizens of the world. But that obligation—to be a citizen of the world—may not always require travel. What it does require is imagination.

More trustworthy and reputable sources than Spiro Agnew have noted the resemblances that eventually strike the traveler. Calvino's Marco Polo, for one: "Travelling, you realize that differences are lost; each city takes to resembling all cities, places exchange their form, order, distances, a shapeless dust cloud invades the continents." In his case the resemblances are not surprising, for the invisible cities Calvino has Marco Polo visit are dreams, dreams of Venice, all of them, a Venice transmogrified through a series of prisms into one fantastical city after another, existing only in the imagination.

borders or *cabo tormentoso*

T HE LANDLORDS of our apartment in Rome during the year of Harry's Fulbright grant took a shine to us, their young American tenants. They were a couple in their fifties called Vittorio and Vera Roselli—we called them Signor Vito and Signora Vera—and they lived with Signora Vera's mother, whom we called Signora, and with a dog called Roxy. Because we were fairly new to Italy—it was our second trip there—we couldn't quite place them, though the formal terms of address implied that they were old-fashioned, rather conservative. Their draped apartment exuded darkness and heaviness. Airy apartments with unshielded windows and light-weight furniture imply that the occupants are open to whatever the fresh air might blow in. Closed, weighty apartments allude to ages past and suggest an unwillingness to open the windows of the spirit. The Rosellis' dim rooms had dense dun-colored arm-chairs and dark carpets. Even the dog, Roxy, was dun-colored and slouched around with a heavy tread. He ate heavy food; they fed him lasagna and other pasta dishes, which I suppose is no odder than Americans feeding their dogs hamburgers or bits of steak, but it seemed odd to one as untraveled—back then—as I that a dog would eat lasagna. The dog spoke, or rather understood, Italian, naturally, and this too felt peculiar. At first I would address him, insofar as I addressed him at all, in English, until I saw he had no idea what I was talking about.

Despite their apartment's heaviness and darkness, the Rosellis were a merry family; they laughed a lot. Plump Signora Vera was positively bubbly, with her bouncing blonde curls. Signor Vito, egg-shaped, had a broad, red-cheeked face and was loquacious in a hoarse breathy voice, though we didn't always grasp all he said. The older Signora spoke very little but smiled placidly much of the time and went about in a long gray woolen cardigan in all seasons.

Because Italian social life was an enigma and because our friendship was evolving in a language we didn't totally grasp, we had no idea what Signor Vito did for a living (aside from renting out our apartment, which surely couldn't sustain a family) or how educated they were or what kind of friends they had—in short, who they were. But they were kind. Now and then they invited us over for dinner. The dining room was lit by many small fussy lamps. What we ate and what we found to talk about I cannot recall. I do recall that at the close of every evening, along with the good nights at the door, Signor Vito would say cheerfully, "*Tante belle cose.*" I wasn't sure at first what this meant. That is, I knew that literally it meant "so many beautiful things," and in time I recognized it as simply a benevolent parting phrase— may good things happen to you—like "have a nice day," only less vapid and formulaic. (The inane "have a nice day" actually did not come into vogue until years later.) "*Tante belle cose*" struck me as somehow archaic; no one else we knew used it, and it fit in with the antiquated feel of the Rosellis' apartment. I didn't know what to say in return and only long after did I learn that I should have responded with "*altrettanto,*" same to you.

The Rosellis had a fine, shiny grand piano, and when they learned that I played, they insisted that I come over to practice whenever I wished; they lived just a fifteen-minute walk away, across the Tiber. And so I did that, and was greeted by Signora Vera and her mother and Roxy the dog. Once when I came in the middle of the day, Signora Vera answered the door in her nightgown and robe. I had interrupted the afternoon nap, for which the entire family undressed as if it were night. I would play the piano as long as I liked, undisturbed except sometimes by the polyphonic barking of Roxy.

In the spring they drove us out into the country for a picnic, and insisted on bringing all the food. Italian picnics, or at least the Rosellis' picnics, were not like the American picnics of my youth, with fried chicken and potato salad or sandwiches on paper plates, eaten on a blanket spread out on the grass. The Rosellis brought a large folding table, chairs, china, silverware, linen napkins, wine and wine glasses, lasagna in baking dishes wrapped in aluminum foil, salad, and fruit and cheese for dessert, and we went to what they called their property in the *campagna*, a clearing in the woods where they set out the feast.

The Rosellis were not our only local friends. While we hung out and explored Rome with the other Fulbright scholars and their wives (I can't recall any women Fulbrights with husbands along for company), the friends we enjoyed most were the real Romans who had nothing to do with the Fulbright program. Besides the Rosellis, there was the head of the sanitation department (*Nettezza Urbana*, a phrase we delighted in translating as Urban Neatness; the locutions of a language you barely know seem cute; when you know it better they shed their cuteness). We knew the sanitation chief through his American wife, who'd been the Personnel Director at the American Friends Service Committee in Philadelphia, where I had typed for two years while Harry attended graduate school. They in turn introduced us to a journalist married to a simultaneous translator. I loved hearing the translator tell of the international conferences she worked at because one of my many ongoing fantasies was of being a simultaneous translator, a profession open primarily to those who grew up bilingual, which I did not.

Most of all we were attached to our next-door neighbors, a placid, gracious widow and her three sons, who liked to horse around and asked endless questions about the United States. If our landlords were hard to place, it was very clear who this family was, a working-class family that had lost its husband and father. The mother kept house and cooked while the oldest son, around twenty-one or two, worked in the post office, and the middle one in a shop. The youngest, about fifteen, was still in school. They befriended us when we first moved in and would invite us over in the evening to watch television and sip anisette liqueur. Dropping in on the neighbors that way made us feel we were truly living in Rome and not mere outsiders, sojourning. Once in a while we'd catch an old American movie, always dubbed in Italian so we weren't absolutely sure of the dialogue, and they would ask us to explain the customs or the settings.

Our next-door neighbors had also been friends with the previous occupant of our apartment, one Douglas, an American. They mentioned this Douglas character so often that we grew faintly jealous, as if Douglas had made a profound impression we could not hope to equal. We imagined they missed him and found us a disappointing substitute. They mentioned him often, yet we never managed to find out anything specific, such as where he was from, how old he was, what he did, or why he was in Rome.

So the charm of Douglas was and remains to this day an enigma. I was trying to write fiction during that year in Rome, and besides the abandoned story of the woman who thought of ways of killing her husband, I attempted a story about Douglas, man of mystery, but didn't succeed because I had nothing to go on, nothing to start it off. Today most likely I could write a story without a clue about where to begin, but back then I couldn't. But today Douglas no longer interests me, alas. Frequently by the time we've acquired the means to do something, we've lost the desire. On the other hand, we may have a yen to do something once we've lost the means. I have always wanted to try hang-gliding, but the time when I could muster the nerve to step off a cliff with wings strapped to my back and trust to the air currents is long past. It's hard enough to trust that airplanes will stay aloft.

Ce

The first time I boarded an airplane, with the nonchalance of adolescence, was back in the early days of recreational flying.

Although my parents didn't frequent Miami Beach I had an unexpected chance to see it. My Uncle Bert and Aunt Lily invited me to accompany them there during a school Easter break. I accepted right away. I wanted to explore, and this was the best in the way of exploration that I could hope for just then. I was fifteen. Bert and Lily's older son, my cousin, was a student at the University of Miami and they were going to visit him, to see for themselves how he was living rather than conscript neighbors.

My parents, who considered Miami Beach well within the range of the acceptable, practically a sister city, and knowing my bent for the exotic—in short supply in Brooklyn—gave their permission. They trusted that my aunt and uncle knew something about travel because Bert and Lily were the only family members who ventured beyond the borders of the known world. They took cruises and went on tours to faraway places. To my mother, this was a form of eccentricity or self-punishment. Long after our trip to Florida, well into old age, my aunt and uncle continued traveling. At the announcement of each new trip, my mother would shake her head ruefully and sigh with pity for my aunt, who she believed was dragged along against her wishes. Maybe she was right. Or maybe travel was part of an informal pre-nuptial agreement. My aunt was a docile woman who rarely disagreed with her husband, in public, at any rate. She appreciated the comfortable life he made possible for her, even if in return she had to put up with his wanderlust, his vile temper, and uncensored tongue.

The plan was that Bert and Lily would drive down to Miami and I would be sent by plane along with their other son, Phil, a year and a half younger than I, who even at thirteen had the long, sallow, intimidating but handsome face of a number of men in the family; the others had broad, flat faces, almost Asian, suggesting some of their forebears had traveled quite far. In those days people used to dress for a flight as if for a job interview—dignified, businesslike clothing. I wore a gray suit with stockings and Cuban heels, squat two inch heels that have lately become stylish but at the time were considered appropriate for teen-agers, not sexy like the four-inch spike heels I couldn't wait to wear, but still denoting a level slightly above childhood. I can't remember what my cousin Phil wore, which is just as well because during the flight I threw up on my suit and on whatever he had on. There was always a coolness between us after that.

I saw Miami Beach with its famed luxury hotels. Typically, I remember little of the trip. Among my few misty memories are several outings to places with performing animals—dolphins, alligators—many meals in Junior's, my uncle's violent temper and my aunt's meekness. For this I did not need to travel. I witnessed it often enough in Brooklyn. You never knew what might set him off, a waitress's delay in bringing his lunch, say, and for this reason it was embarrassing to eat in restaurants with him.

Later on, when I was grown, my mother revealed that she had been courted by Bert, who made the tactical error of introducing her to his younger brother, who became my father. My father was the youngest in that family of nine children, but his ranking was often in dispute because the four brothers (a fifth, the oldest, had remained in Russia) lied about their age, out of vanity. To listen to them, you would have thought they'd all been born within a few months of each other or been quadruplets. Legend has it that when they registered for the draft, the clerk noted that he already had more than one man from that family born in that year—how was it possible?

My mother never said exactly how far her romance with Bert had progressed, but in any event I was enormously relieved that she chose my father over him. No doubt she was too, in light of all the traveling that would have been in store. My father's temperament was also irascible and hard to take, but not quite so vitriolic as Bert's, and my father was better-natured. On the other hand Bert made a lot of money, though had I been his daughter I would probably have had to spend my legacy on psychiatrists.

My mother, always confident about her charms, hinted that Bert still had a soft spot for her but I never detected anything of the kind. I never detected any soft spots at all. As a pair, they would have been painfully mismatched. "Whoever is stiff and inflexible," says the *Tao te Ching*, "is a disciple of death. Whoever is soft and yielding is a disciple of life." My mother, soft and yielding, would have contended with Bert all her life—divorce, in that time and place, being virtually unthinkable except under the most egregious of pressures: crime, blatant or incessant adultery, rampant alcoholism, none of which were Bert's vices. Travel would not have qualified. If I told her of friends of mine who were getting divorced, she refused to understand why. "He doesn't drink, he doesn't gamble, he doesn't run around, so what's the trouble?" That sort of throwback aphorism might suggest she was oblivious to the infinite nuances of human relationship. She was exquisitely sensitive to those nuances. She just didn't consider them, however blighted, as grounds for divorce.

"The hard and stiff will be broken. The soft and supple will prevail," the verse continues, but this is not always true. Bert lived way into his nineties, imposing his will until the very end.

In our small Miami Beach hotel or rooming house we occupied two rooms, for propriety. I slept in one room with my aunt while my uncle and cousin shared the other. It would have been awkward for my thirteen-year-old cousin and me to room together, especially after I had thrown up on him. At fifteen I didn't know much but I did know that married people liked to sleep together, and I wondered if Bert and Lily felt deprived. I felt mildly guilty at being the cause of their temporary celibacy. At night, going to bed, my aunt and I sometimes discussed my uncle's fits of temper and what scene or scenes they had generated that day. These conversations must have been at my instigation. I can't imagine her ever bringing the subject up. I asked why she didn't answer him back. I was speaking from the example of my own parents; my father yelled and screamed but my mother answered back. My aunt said fearfully that she didn't know what he might do: he might hit her. I could have told her that those types didn't hit, at least judging by my father, but I didn't go that far. I just regarded her with mute pity.

I also felt sorry for her because I could see, through her transparent white nightgown, that her hips bumped out and then her thighs bumped out, with a kind of vertical valley in between. From my waist to my upper thighs was one gentle curve and I did not wish this to alter with age. Of course I had seen my mother's body many times, but she was fat so there were no valleys or indentations anywhere. My aunt was slim. This too I did not bring up for discussion.

We visited my older cousin and walked around the campus of his university. He invited me—I don't know if this was his idea or if his parents urged him—to a pool party one night with his college friends. In the sultry Miami Beach night everyone cavorted

around the lit-up pool in bathing suits. I wore a royal blue vel-
veteen bathing suit I had inherited from my older sister. I had
coveted this bathing suit for quite some time and when I put it
on I couldn't stop admiring myself in the mirror. But almost none
of the college kids, certainly none of the boys, spoke to me, and
I ambled about on the edge of the party in my beautiful bathing
suit, drinking soda and retreating underwater until it was merci-
fully over. I was drenched with awkwardness but also relieved, for
I didn't know what I would have said had any boys approached
me. I didn't know how to flirt even with boys my own age, and
these were college boys. I was glad to be back with Phil, with
whom I could behave like an older woman.

This was hardly the first time I endured that vertiginous sense
of boundless alienation. I'd known it ever since I could remember,
although in childhood I wouldn't have known the word, any more
than I would have known the expression "bad faith." Not belonging, I would have called it, or not fitting in. In my innocence, or
child wisdom, I must have thought it was a commonplace feeling
everyone shared, something that came along with the package of
life, like hunger or boredom. The only time I was completely free
of it was when I was alone. I belonged with myself; that much I
knew for sure.

Allen Shawn writes similarly about anxiety as a built-in, "natural" condition, in his memoir of a lifetime of agoraphobia, *Wish
I Could Be There*. To Shawn, going anywhere produces enormous
anxiety along with elaborate coping mechanisms, and in his book
he goes to heroic lengths to study and deconstruct the nature of
his fear. He quotes a commentator on the French philosopher
Lacan who suggests that

anxiety is not a 'defense' at all, but rather the very foundation upon which we erect our fragile sense of self. Thus it
is not that anxiety conceals a truth (as Freud suggested),
but rather that lying beneath the constructs we use to cre-
ate a sense of order, control, and selfhood, anxiety is the
truth. . . . To Lacan, anxiety is therefore the fear that the
self will be unmasked as a falsehood.

With my family and friends, or at school, I belonged, yes,
but never entirely, without reservation. A part of me was always
looking on, mildly puzzled, wondering what I was doing in this
unlikely group. If my self was a falsehood, surely their selves were
as well. Even more so, I thought in my arrogance. Then when
I realized the feeling had a name, like an ailment, I understood
that it was perhaps not endemic to being alive, that it need not be
perpetual or universal. And so I felt faintly guilty about harboring
it, as if I were ungrateful for the relatively privileged niche that
destiny had assigned me.

So I was on intimate terms with not belonging. It was like not
fitting comfortably into your skin—an existential itch or tug at the
seams of the self. You want to shed your skin for something more
comfortable, like throwing off your fancy clothes and tight shoes
on coming home from a formal dinner with strangers. You long
to be more profoundly at home as well—emotionally, psychologi-
cally home. But where is that safe haven? If we don't carry it with
us, it's nowhere.

Even in the more literal sense, "home," where one belongs,
as opposed to "away," is hard to define. How far does home, the
physical and cultural comfort zone, extend? A twenty-mile radius
from where we live, or where we were born? A hundred miles? Is

it wherever we speak the language? For those easeful souls who do carry their safety within, maybe the entire universe? The expanse of where we belong, or feel we belong, can change depending on circumstances. When I'm at home in New York City for a long period, any place west of Pennsylvania or south of Washington can feel alien. On the other hand, when I'm in a far country and feeling uneasy in my skin, I'd be grateful to be transported to Wyoming or Idaho or anywhere in my native country.

The feeling of where home is can be bred in the bone or blood. I met a young artist not long ago who told me she was adopted as an infant by a rural, uneducated family in Louisiana. Although they raised her lovingly, she never felt at home. She had a talent for drawing and painting, and cultivated the fantasy that her birth parents were figures from the art world in New York City—whether this was based on any clues other than her own gifts I don't know. As an adult, when she came to New York to settle, she felt instantly at home.

The evening at the pool in Miami Beach was the first time I experienced not belonging culturally, in the context of travel to a new place. That felt more justified. I was not different because of an obscure, maybe shameful, weakness or flaw. I was objectively different: this place, these people, this weather, these customs had no connection to who or what I was. Pool parties! In March!

On later travels, when this feeling assailed me, I invented fantasies to make the time pass more tolerably. I was in exile because of some disruption taking place in my home country—maybe I was an outspoken political dissident at risk of imprisonment for my heedless words. Or I was suspected of being a terrorist because I had unwittingly given money to the wrong organization. When reason and calm returned to my native land, I would be welcomed back; meanwhile I must be patient and endure. Or I was on an important secret mission for my government, which required that I play the role of tourist while gathering essential information and making contacts. That fantasy gave me what I lacked, a sense of purpose, a task woven into the unfamiliar tapestry of daily life abroad.

But notwithstanding exile or secret missions, and though the trip might be past its halfway mark—the laundry accumulating, the vitamin pills dwindling—still, still, every single moment must be lived. There's no eluding the instant, whether at home or away. We're often urged to live in the present moment, and so I do. But that much-vaunted skill has its drawbacks: each moment is a fractal of eternity—heaven or hell, depending on where, for the moment, you're consigned. Clichés can placate us—time is the great healer, you'll get through it, and so on—but it is still time. It can't be skipped over, only endured. What is that process of getting through, inch by inch, between *now* and some future, better, *then*? How does it feel, what is its texture? When I focus on it in this way, I realize that those overlooked interstices are what I've chosen to write about so often in fiction.

Anxiety informs the only other vivid memory from my Florida trip, but anxiety of a more domestic, reasonable nature. My uncle periodically let Phil steer the car—a prelude to teaching him how to drive—but not sit in the driver's seat. He would have Phil lean over from the passenger seat to steer. I was not a nervous passenger, having grown up with my father's bold and excellent driving, but this antic, which went on for long stretches on endless roads leading to the various animal performances, struck me as extremely unwise. My aunt and I sat in the back seat. Like her, I was tense and silent. I would go home soon, I thought, if Phil's steering didn't kill us. My ordeal would be over, but she had to spend her whole life this way.

Cle

If Miami Beach did not quite live up to the glamour I craved, at least it was not the Catskills. The Catskills do not bear writing about, as least for me they do not. Others have done it. A literature of Catskills nostalgia has sprung up, proliferating in inverse relation to the Catskills' decline as a summer resort. Not only literature but films, too, have managed to glamorize a kind of hungry, rapacious vulgarity—witness *Dirty Dancing*.

I resisted the Catskills from a tender age. Going there—a three-hour drive in a car packed with blankets and bed linens—seemed less a form of travel than a transposition of daily life from an urban setting to a duller, mountainous one. The only differences between the Catskills and the life I knew in Brooklyn were landscape and climate. Trees and fresh country air were not what moved me. I was looking for small subtle shifts in temperament and style and modes of life. I knew there were ways of living other than what flourished on the Brooklyn streets, but they couldn't be found in the Catskills.

Aside from the social conformity and the crushing mountain greenery, another disadvantage of the Catskills was that they were far from water—I don't count the various lakes and swimming holes. I mean real water, an ocean. To be near water I find essential; it is the edge, the place of escape. It's also the great unifier, a reminder of what the world is made of. It is the place of no artificial boundaries, no gates or fences or official border crossings set up as they are on land.

Borders in general are a source of difficulty as well as pointless labor for government bureaucrats, not to mention anguish for the people who wish to cross them, or who do cross them only to find misery different from the kind they fled. Whenever I hear yet another news report about the nonsensical contortions, both semantic and political, of our government in its attempts to legislate immigration, I wonder why we need borders at all. This may sound patently absurd, given the state of the world. It would take a planetary revolution of the most drastic kind to undo our system of nation states and border controls. I am aware of that. And yet the national borders in Europe and Africa, for example, are a relatively recent development, when seen in the vast trail of human history. There is the added irony that at a time when Europe is relaxing the notion of strict borders— witness the European Union and the attendant ease of crossing borders—the United States is busy building fences and deploying armed guards.

As practically absurd as a borderless world might sound, it is equally absurd that certain residents of a place should be "legal" and others "illegal." Besides "illegal" people, borders make possible invasions, occupations, detentions, prisons, and so many other evils. Why shouldn't people come and go freely on the face of the earth? At least as freely as money and corporate investments, which are rarely detained at borders.

The artificiality and senselessness of borders are vivid whenever we cross one. I pass a checkpoint and am suddenly in Canada, where the scenery looks the same as it did fifty feet back, the language sounds the same and the people look the same. On the other hand, I stand in line to have my passport stamped in Mexico and suddenly I've crossed the border. The signs are in another language, the shops and streets and houses look poorer and shabbier than they did fifty feet back; there is a heavier despair in the ambience. Why should there be poverty and wretchedness on one side of an arbitrary line and prosperity on the other?

Beyond entrenched customs and elaborate regulations, terrorism, today, is the primary justification for strict border control. But there has been terrorism in the United States perpetrated by Americans. And the Saudis who carried out the September 11 attacks were not stopped by border regulations. Since then, home-grown terrorist cells (of doubtful motives and capacities) have been discovered within our borders. Safety from terrorism does not depend on efficient borders. Even if it did, fear can hardly be the most salutary motive in determining national policy.

The other obvious argument against my fantasy of a borderless world is that everyone would rush to certain places, the United States, for one. I suspect that tide of hopeful immigrants would subside quickly. Already we are no longer as desirable a destination as we once were. It is worth noting that if the essentials of life, such as food, were distributed according to need, and if the profits from third-world investments were apportioned justly, the numbers of "illegals" would level off. Fewer people would want or need to leave their places of origin.

But to return from this impossible fantasy to the openness of water: given our attachment to arbitrary separations, water, like land, must be represented on maps and assigned a name. And given the nature of water, setting its exact borders must be problematic. Nations lay claim to their contiguous waters and extend their borders far into them. A couple of years ago Iran held captive fifteen British sailors who they said had trespassed into Iranian waters. The British denied the charge. Each side had photographs to support its position. Lives hung in the balance and international relations tottered, all over an invisible line drawn in a fluid medium.

Visitors to the Cape of Good Hope at the southern tip of Africa are promised the thrill of standing on a craggy peak and seeing two oceans at once, the Atlantic to the west and the Indian to the east. I was excited to see this famously dangerous place—especially from the tourist's safe vantage point, a fenced-in platform on the edge of the cliff, a sheer drop to the roiling turbulence below. Those waters have been lethal. In the fifteenth century, countless sailors met their deaths trying to round the Cape's stormy corner. In 1488, the Portuguese explorer Bartolomeu Dias finally managed it, opening up a trading route between Europe and Asia. *Cabo Tormentoso*, Dias called it: Cape of Storms. He went along for the ride in 1497 when Vasco da Gama rounded the Cape. Then in 1500, not having learned to let well enough alone, Dias went on a third trip but died in one of the region's infamous storms. The captain of the eighteenth-century ship, *The Flying Dutchman* fared even worse. He rashly declared that he would round the stormy Cape no matter what, even if it took till Judgment Day. According to legend, he's still trying. Sightings have been reported over the centuries, most recently in 1942.

King John II of Portugal soon changed *Cabo Tormentoso* to the Cape of Good Hope, a name that better reflected the general exhilaration at the prospect of reaching the East. It's also a name more likely to attract tourists, who today arrive in busloads. Before they climb to the rocky, raw tip of the Cape, though, they often meet up with the local baboons who congregate near the snack bar and have learned to snatch sandwiches from visitors' hands and nimbly undo their cellophane wrappers. The baboons also frequent the parking lot, where they squat on the roofs of cars, munching and waiting to greet the drivers.

Looking south from the tip of the Cape, to your right is the Atlantic Ocean, to your left the Indian. Given my love of oceans, this was a bonanza, regardless of what they were called. But of course there can be no precise border where one ocean turns into the next, no line drawn in the water like a line in the sand. The waters mingle. They flow into each other, back and forth, untroubled by any border control, and who can say which sea is which or where their names and ripples change?

Just so, it is probably arbitrary to distinguish my stay-at-home self from my traveling self. Or from the self Camus says is returned to us by travel, or the one I say is made comatose by travel. The self doesn't exist as a fixed entity; it can't be pinned down or bounded. Like the cat in the hat, it spreads and shrinks from moment to moment, according to its container—context—and its need. One might say we can generate selves infinitely—we don't know our own strength, as it were. Or our own mutability.

It follows that we needn't always travel to have the experience of travel, and we don't always leave our selves—or souls—en route. When Kublai Khan remarks to Marco Polo, "I do not know when you have had time to visit all the countries you describe to me. It seems to me you have never moved from this garden," the inveterate traveler replies:

> Everything I see and do assumes meaning in a mental space where the same calm reigns as here. . . . At the moment when I concentrate and reflect, I find myself again, always, in this garden, at this hour of the evening, in your august presence, though I continue, without a moment's pause, moving up a river green with crocodiles or counting the barrels of salted fish being lowered into the hold.

Where is Marco Polo really? Has he truly "never moved from this garden?" If so, Calvino suggests that staying put and dreaming can be as adventurous and as illuminating as wandering. And that the imagination can conjure up a tangible world as easily as the mind constructs a labyrinth of words, seemingly wayward but leading inevitably towards a center. Or perhaps Marco Polo is constantly on the move, taking his entire self with him, achieving the ideal mingling of home self and travel self, dreaming self and the one who moves in the actual world.

Ce

However we read Calvino's riddle, it's undeniable that the mind takes its own trips, and that sedentary travel yields plenty of curiosities. Looking for de Maistre's *Journey Around My Bedroom*, for instance, meant traveling by mouse around the library's computer, which led me fortuitously to another book listed right beneath it: *A Journey Around My Skull*, by the twentieth-century Hungarian author, Frigyes Karinthy, a book so obscure that the Columbia University Reserve Room had only one copy, which could not be removed from the premises. (In 2008, this work of Karinthy's was reissued in a paperback edition.) And yet Karinthy, whom I'd never heard of, was one of the most prolific and popular authors in Hungary in the last century. We in the United States are appallingly ignorant of much of the world's literature, partly because so relatively few translations appear in English. Publishers worry—needlessly, I think—that translations will deter readers, and as a result we're far more isolated than we realize, despite our huge capital investments all over the globe.

Because of the arbitrariness of any system organized by the alphabet, *A Journey Around My Skull* was listed among the travel books, but it turned out to have nothing to do with literal travel at all. It is an autobiographical account of brain surgery performed while the patient—our narrator—is wide awake.

Karinthy is forty-seven years old when the ominous signs appear. He has auditory hallucinations, hears rumbling noises like trains pulling out of stations, has periods of forgetting who and where he is; he imagines inanimate objects moving around his room; he suffers dizzy spells and pains in the back of his head; he veers around when he walks and his handwriting gets jiggly and illegible. It is 1938. Europe is on the verge of war. The news reports are as surreal as the hallucinations, an outward reflection of Karinthy's private affliction. He fancies himself ruling over a dominion of cells and organs that have erupted in rebellion. Or else he's a ship's captain beset by the crew's mutiny.

His wife is a neurologist. Around the time his symptoms begin—before they become horribly persistent, before he takes them seriously—he drops in to see her at the hospital where she works. There he notices a patient with a brain tumor and remarks frivolously, Maybe I too have a brain tumor.

Wouldn't you know it? After several misdiagnoses, it's determined that Karinthy does have a brain tumor and needs surgery right away, or else he'll go blind or be paralyzed or die. Here is where the account, thus far suave and witty—Karinthy comes across as an urbane European flaneur suddenly twitching and stumbling on the streets of Budapest, a kind of Hungarian Jacques Tati—ventures into the metaphysical.

> I know that the idea in my mind was an insane delusion and my education and scientific instinct rose up to protest against it, but . . . I could not rid myself of the notion that my trouble began only when I spoke about it. Not only was it born at that moment, but as a direct result of my having given it a name. I felt that things happened because we gave names to them, and thus came to look upon them as possibilities. Everything we regard as possible comes to pass. Reality is the child of man's imagination.

Precisely that same mental leap is made by Tolstoi's protagonist in *The Death of Ivan Ilyich*. The sick man persuades himself that his stomach cancer erupted when he banged his side, hanging curtains in his drawing room. "Can it be true that here, on this drapery, as at the storming of a bastion, I lost my life? How awful and how stupid! It just can't be! It can't be, yet it is." The imagination will go to any lengths to assure us that we have some control over a dread illness. Provoking one's own doom is better than being powerless against unaccountable, mindless matter. So reason devises myths to explain the body's treachery, just as the myths of ancient gods explain the treacheries life foists on us.

To allay his fright, Karinthy next thinks that his brain tumor might have intentions, purposes he could decipher.

> Perhaps this mysterious tumor, despite its apparent work of destruction, . . . wanted to become something which would turn out eventually to man's advantage, but for the present wished its purpose unknown. Or it may have set out with the intention of becoming a constructive agent, but had forgotten its original purpose or proved unable to carry it out, perhaps for lack of the necessary means. Or maybe the central government did not allow it to achieve its object.

Whatever the tumor's intentions, it clearly has to go. The day of the operation arrives, coincidentally the same day Italian troops invade Addis Ababa in Ethiopia. Karinthy's head is shaved. He feels probes invading his skull to obtain fluid. Thanks to a local anesthetic, he has no pain, but he feels everything: the incision made in his skull, his scalp being peeled back to expose the bare bone, the breaking of the bones. This was what anyone undergoing brain surgery in 1938 had to endure; allegedly the risks of death or error were reduced by twenty-five percent if the patient remained awake. Karinthy feels everything and resists with all his might, to no avail. Now and then the surgeons murmur a few encouraging words and he replies, but nothing he says can stop their journey. Only in the last hour of many does he lose consciousness, then wakes to confusion, raving, delirium.

In the end he recovers completely, enough to write the book about "my burgled brain," a precursor of the current genre of "illness narratives" and more entertaining than many of its successors.

Karinthy's ordeal is one of those stories that makes us thankful to be living in the twenty-first century, or at least after the advent of anesthesia. This gratitude may not be warranted. An April 2006 article in *The New York Times Magazine* describes a "radical new brain surgery for depression" involving deep brain stimulation, which doctors hope will be used more widely. It's already been tested on a handful of patients whose depressions resisted the usual treatments of drugs, psychotherapy, and electroshock. Like Karinthy, patients receive only a local anesthetic; they are kept awake

> so they can describe any changes. . . . The surgical team shaves much of the patient's head and attaches to the skull, with four screws drilled through skin into bone, the stereotactic frame that will hold the head steady against the operating table and serve as a navigational aid. . . . "You can't truly feel it," as one patient said, "but you can hear it and see it and smell it."

In the operation described in the article, once the frame was in place, the doctor drilled into the top of the patient's skull, sent the electrodes down through a tube and planted them in the brain, attached the leads to a pacemaker in the patient's chest, and turned on the juice. The patient immediately felt some lifting of her depression. So our modern miracles become a higher-tech repetition of history. And the mind's borders, its surfaces and depths, remain no less troublesome and mysterious than those of the globe.

clerical work

IF WE BELIEVE that Marco Polo "never moved from this garden," then the cultivated imagination is a more powerful vehicle than any that runs on fuel. But even if the imagination is weak, adventure may still be near at hand. All it takes, beyond a willing spirit, is a change of season and occupation. The most memorable summer, during my early stretch of enforced vacations in the Catskills, was the summer I refused to make the trip. I insisted on staying in the city with my father. The fathers of families who went to the mountains worked in the city all week and drove up on Friday nights for a conjugal visit, to return, revitalized, on Sunday night. The more ardent, or idle, drove up Thursday night and left Monday morning; my father was sometimes among them. My parents agreed to let me stay in the city and I was freed from the unending mountain greenery.

I had never spent a summer in the city. I imagined it to be exotic, and the exotic was what I longed for: tropically languid ambience, air hushed and dense, buildings swooning with heat, deserted streets with occasional husbands wandering about forlorn. I got a job in Manhattan by lying about my age. My father and I ate out every night, since neither of us could cook. My father's cooking began and ended in boyhood, when his mother left him alone and told him to boil an egg for his lunch. Just put it in a pot, she said, and turn on the gas. He did, and the egg exploded; he neglected to add water. As for me, my mother had never taught me anything about cooking. Later she explained that she didn't like to interrupt me when I was reading.

We would drive to a local restaurant; my father would slam the door of the blue DeSoto with his usual vehemence and stride towards the entrance, his suit unwilted despite the heat, his briefcase swinging from his hand in a snappy arc. A man of the world. This was how he must look every summer, without us, I realized. I had pictured him, quite mistakenly, as desolate. Apparently people could live without elaborate domestic trappings. In the restaurants we ate things my mother did not cook: shrimp, clams, and lobster every night. My father liked watching me savor the forbidden foods, like a roué introducing a young virgin to uncommon delights. Sometimes we went to air-conditioned movies afterwards, and no one cared what time we got home. He was a different sort of father on those summer evenings, calmer and mellow; gone were the tantrums and the perpetual air of irritation. Weather and solitude slowed him down. Maybe, like me, he enjoyed the release from family life, although he was always eager to drive back up to the mountains for the weekend.

I think my mother expected I would tire of the heat, the job, the crowded subways, and would hurry back to the mountains, but I never did tire of the city in summer. It was as fine as I had dreamed: hot, sultry, slow, and seductive. If I had known at the time about the *Tao te Ching* and its counsel of non-doing ("Practice not-doing, and everything will fall into place"), I might have been tempted to think it was right there, in the slow haze of the city summer, but I would have been wrong.

The subtle Taoist notion of non-doing is nothing like dreamy languidness. Nor should it be mistaken for defeatism, throwing up the hands against responsibility or decisive action, closing the door on the frenetic intrusions of the world. The commentators agree this is hardly what Lao-tzu meant, but none puts it so well and simply as Stephen Mitchell. He compares non-doing to the miraculous ease of the athlete whose movement appears to happen on its own, so carefully has he trained and so implicitly can he trust his body. Imagine Michael Jordan nonchalantly allowing the ball to waft through the basket, or a ballet dancer doing thirty-two pirouettes, seemingly propelled and sustained by the air around her. He might have used the example of great musicians as well. Or of Matisse near the end of his life, making his swirling cut-outs while bedridden and in pain, guiding the scissors with ripened ease. After a lifetime of drawing with pen or charcoal he didn't even have to look down at the paper, according to his biographer, Hilary Spurling: "He said he had been mistaken all his life in measuring the significance of any given work by the struggles that went into it."

> Less and less do you need to force things,
> until finally you arrive at non action.
> When nothing is done,
> nothing is left undone.

Of this paradox, Mitchell writes, "Nothing is done because the doer has wholeheartedly vanished into the deed; the fuel has been completely transformed into flame. This 'nothing' is, in fact, everything."

The Stephen Mitchell translation has been disparaged in some quarters, probably because it is too "accessible" to unscholarly readers. Ursula Le Guin, whose own luminous translation—or "rendition," as she calls it—is the closest to poetry and the most idiosyncratic, calls Mitchell's "not useful," a discreet put-down from someone who grew up with the book. As a child, she saw her father studying it over and over, and she nourished a lifelong attachment to it.

Mitchell's translation does in fact have a California, human-potential-movement cast, but it is limpid and lucid and my friend and I developed an affection for it even though we are not in the least California types and are even purists in our way. It is infused with a winning felicity and makes gymnastic leaps over chasms of enigma or ambiguity. If Le Guin's success comes from childhood intimacy, Mitchell's trapeze-artist sureness might be due to his fourteen-year training in Zen Buddhism, which must have served him equally well in his translations of Rilke's poetry and *The Book of Job*. "If I haven't always translated Lao-tzu's words," he writes, "my intention has always been to translate his mind." Which is the task of any writer—to translate, transfer, transliterate: literally bring something across the chasm between inner and outer, the intangibles of thought, feeling and sensibility into the auditory medium of words.

The job I took, the summer when I refused to go to the Catskills, was in an office. The only other work I could think of was babysitting, which didn't appeal to me. It wasn't work that produced anything, I thought at sixteen; it wasn't part of the great world but the small, the world I wanted to flee, the world in which my mother did her shopping and cleaning and cooking—also not work, as I then conceived it.

I wanted to be in the world of genuine work, wherever it was my father went each morning dressed in a suit and tie and swinging his briefcase. The great world, as I imagined it, was offices, for I knew my father had an office somewhere, though I also knew he didn't spend much time in it; instead he went around to other people's offices, paying house calls, balancing their books and figuring out their taxes. And so I found a job in the Purchasing Department at Popular Science Publishing Company, located near Madison Square in New York City.

To get the job I said I was eighteen. I sat in a small room with four desks and no windows. The other desks were occupied by Lucille, a dark, perky, tough-looking girl with pock-marked skin who also claimed to be eighteen and was probably telling the truth, and two men about thirty, one tall and fair and shambly in a creased white shirt and off-center tie, the other small, dark-haired, neat and domesticated, both destined, or so I imagined, for a lifetime of clerical work, though of a more elevated nature than mine.

I would not be there for life because I was going to college in the fall, and I felt mildly sorry for the two men at the same time as I was awed by their greater responsibilities, whatever they were. Our boss was a volatile tyrant named Mary F., whom I grew to loathe. I have only loathed a handful of people in my life. The other loathings have long since dissipated but this one remains firm (even though loathing is far from the spirit of the *Tao te Ching*). Mary F.'s training strategy was mockery. She hinted at terrible punishments that would come my way if I made any mistakes. The worst moment in my tenure at Popular Science, which published the eponymous magazine as well as *Popular Mechanics*, magazines in which I had no interest whatsoever, came when I made an error typing a purchase order. Purchase orders came in quadruplicate, each sheet a different pastel color, with slippery carbons in between. If you made a mistake you had to carefully erase it on each of the thin pastel sheets, which tore easily. The figure I should have typed was 3,000, whether pounds or reams of paper I can't remember and most likely didn't know back then either. I typed 30,000. When Mary F. discovered my error she erupted in a tantrum. Her face clouded over, her jaw stiffened, her skirts quivered. "Do you realize what would happen if this order went through? They would print ten times as many magazines as we need."

I didn't care how many magazines got printed; what I minded was being yelled at. I grew up listening to my father's loud shouting and hated it. I didn't answer Mary F. but assumed an abject expression, thinking that would be the quickest way to make her stop. But as I should have known, people who are prone to tantrums don't stop until they run down, like a car alarm.

During the two weeks when Mary F. went on vacation I took her place as assistant to her boss, Mr. E., a jovial, fair-haired, round-faced man with a Swedish accent who struck me as wise and aged but who was probably around forty-five. A rosy Santa

Claus figure in a seersucker suit, he was always good-humored and never scolded. The dread that coated my skin slipped off like a caul, and I wished fervently that Mary F. would have a fatal accident and never return, but my wish was not granted. No doubt there are ways to handle bullies like Mary F. Today, with the study of behavioral psychology so refined, there must be an entire branch devoted to tactics for disarming petty tyrants. But I was sixteen years old; it was long before I would begin to think in terms of tactics, longer still before I read the *Tao te Ching*, which says, "What is a good man but a bad man's teacher? What is a bad man but a good man's job?" This utopian advice would be hard to carry out in any circumstances and at any age. I was not prepared to be Mary F.'s teacher or to take her on as my job. All I wanted was a clerical job that would save me from the Catskills. All I could think of was to wish her dead.

There were slow periods in the Purchasing Department and I used them to plan my immediate future. I would be going to college in the city because my father judged that I was too immature to live away from home, and besides, he couldn't afford it. I constructed a time chart of my fall activities that included, in addition to college classes, acting and dance classes. I had put aside writing, utterly forgetting the unfinished mystery novel about the twins, one dead (her body found in a hotel room) and one alive. Now I was planning to be an actress. I would continue to play the piano and would also check out horseback riding in Central Park. On my chart I filled in every time slot, exactly the way our school programs had been filled out in high school. I spent hours dreaming of my busy future. I must have been dreaming this way when I typed the extra zero on the purchase order.

Aside from those hours of daydreaming, what I liked about the job was traveling there on the subway from Brooklyn every morning at eight and returning at five, crushed by hordes of fellow workers. This is the great world, I thought. I also liked going out to lunch. Some days I would bring a sandwich and others I would buy a hot dog from a stand on the street. My father didn't ask what I ate for lunch, as my mother would have. She would not have been happy about the hot dogs, which floated for hours, maybe days, in their tank of briny water. Oddly enough, in leafing through travel guides for visitors to the United States, I recently found this explanation of their name in *101 American Customs: Understanding American Language and Culture Through Common Practices*:

> Frankfurters were sold in the United States under the name of "dachshund sausages." . . . They were sold by men who kept them in hot-water tanks. . . . One day a cartoonist drew a cartoon of the sausage depicting a dachshund in a roll. Since he didn't know how to spell 'dachshund' he wrote 'Get Your Hot Dog!' as a caption under the cartoon. Thus, the American hot dog was born.

Lunch hours were part of the grown-up world. At noon in Madison Square Park, among the other workers, I would sit on a bench every day with a book. One day a man with a clipboard approached my bench and inquired if he might ask me a few questions. I was glad to oblige even though my mother had warned me not to talk to strange men. He was taking a survey about people's tastes in coffee. While I munched my hot dog he asked me many questions about how much coffee I drank, whether I liked it dark or light, with sugar or not, and so on. I never drank coffee, but coffee was indisputably part of the grown-up world, so I answered all his questions with great earnestness and he wrote down all my lies, which became part of the world's coffee-drinking statistics. Perhaps they even had some influence on the much later genesis of Starbucks and lattes in their many sizes.

Despite the misery Mary F. caused, I loved the idea of working and earning money. Once in a while I spent my money on clothes in expensive shops on nearby Fifth Avenue. I bought a wool skirt for thirty-four dollars in a tiny French boutique called La Parisienne. The saleswoman had a lilting French accent and treated me with amused deference and said *ooh-la-la* when I emerged from the dressing room wearing the skirt. Making this purchase on my own in a French shop was thrilling; with such a gesture I was undeniably part of the great world. I pictured myself wearing it to school in the fall. Over the weekend I went to the Catskills with my father, and when I reported on my purchase my mother was angry. She said thirty-four dollars was far too much to spend on a skirt. It was almost a week's salary. But I loved the skirt, twirly, dark green and nubby, with red and brown flecks, and I wore it for years, towards the end of its life out of guilt, to amortize it.

I was so entranced by the idea of working and earning money that instead of quitting at the end of the summer I asked for part-time work that I could do while I attended college, even though this would mean revising my activity charts. I was moved to the bookkeeping department and released from Mary F. I sat in a large open area with other clerks, where my new boss, Miss Romanoff, was a tyrant of a different sort. Maybe she was a descendant of the family of Russian Czars deposed in 1917. Miss Romanoff had a bleached blonde page boy, was heavily made up—cheeks rouged

in pink circles and tight red lips against a chalky background—
and walked stiffly in high heels, with tiny steps, as if she were
wearing a lead corset. She had a speech impediment with heavily
dentalized *d*'s and *t*'s, but mostly she was silent, a silence nearly
as intimidating as Mary F.'s tantrums. I was used to tantrums but
unused to silence as a mode of aggression. Miss Romanoff paced
among us, threading her way between the desks like a matron in a
reform school, and under her relentless gaze we worked steadily,
hardly ever raising our heads.

I added up columns of figures in a huge ledger. I didn't know
what they meant but I knew the two facing pages had to tally.
When they didn't, when they were off by even a few pennies, Miss
Romanoff kept me at my desk, looming over me, until I found the
error. Sometimes this made me late for classes.

I continued at Popular Science Publishing Company for two
months into the fall, until the idea of earning money grew sour
under the pancaked gaze of Miss Romanoff. I dropped in at the
Purchasing Department to say good-bye to Lucille and the two
men. They knew I was going to college and I thought they looked
wistful as they watched me leave.

I never did go horseback riding in Central Park. I didn't have
time. It wasn't just a wild notion, however, for I did know how to
ride a horse. I had learned the summer before in the Catskills; the
hotel down the road had a stable. That was one pleasing feature
of the Catskills, going to the hotel stable, climbing onto a horse
and trotting down the dirt roads. Only twice since then have I
ridden a horse—once in the Grand Canyon and once in Jamaica,
when a guide took a group to parts of the island not usually seen
by tourists.

Riding a horse in Jamaica was one way I could escape our compound, a grandiose white hotel festooned with balconies and surrounded by massive iron gates relieved by bursts of color—pink,
orange, and red bougainvillea and hyacinths. When we first drove
up, I saw four guards at the gates, dressed in military uniforms:
khaki shorts and knee socks, and many-pocketed shirts with diagonal leather straps across the chest and holsters at the waist, for
wooden clubs. I had stayed in many hotels in many countries by
that time, but never at one with armed guards.

Our driver had introduced himself as we climbed into his van
at the airport, blinking in the sunlight, carrying our heavy coats,
which had become absurd. "I am Ronald, your driver," he said.
"I was educated in England and so I know what different sorts
of people are like. We are dependent on the tourist trade and so
we treat our visitors very well. We have all kinds here, not only
Americans but Germans, Italians, French."

Once he set off on the dirt road, he turned back every two
minutes to continue his welcome. "We treat our visitors very well,
as I said. Of course there are always a few troublemakers. Thus
the guards, as you will see. We eat goat's meat. Have you ever
tried it? If you like I can take you to a restaurant where they serve
the best goat's meat on the island. Petrol here is very expensive,
seven dollars a gallon. This vehicle, as you can see, was made in
Germany. Do you like our island so far? The sun shines ninety
percent of the time. Our rains are brief, the drops fall slowly. So
slowly you can breathe between the drops. We pride ourselves on
our tradition of friendliness as well as on our sunshine. Ninety

percent of the time. Here is your lovely hotel, have a pleasant stay. Remember, if you want to eat goat's meat, ask for Ronald. Let me shake your hands. Pleasant stay to all."

That was in December of 1980, for Jamaica an election year of intense political strife: two hundred violent deaths, many related to politics. There had been strife since 1972, when the leftist People's National Party, headed by the outspoken Michael Manley, was elected to office, ousting the more conservative, anti-communist Jamaica Labor Party. Manley's progressive policies angered his opponents and made powerful enemies. He was committed to Caribbean solidarity, he excoriated imperialism and the unequal distribution of global wealth, and he had ties with Fidel Castro, none of which pleased the United States or the International Monetary Fund, which Manley held responsible for the island's wretched conditions. Although he managed to nationalize some industry and institute reform in education and housing, the economic crisis grew worse during his term in office, for which he blamed rising oil prices and IMF policies. Unemployment rose and much of the middle class left.

The run-up to the 1980 elections had been especially fraught. In June a plot to overthrow the government was thwarted. Then in October, Manley was defeated and the Jamaica Labor Party reinstated, gratifying to the United States but a blow to progressives, whose hopes for better living conditions and economic independence were disappointed.

In this troubled context, the islanders both depended on tourists and resented them: thus the guards everywhere, protecting the source of revenue. Beneath the smooth smiles of welcome you could glimpse the serrated edge of bitterness.

The first morning, wearing a straw hat against the tropical sun, I set out through the iron gates of the compound. A guard offered to get me a taxi but I said I wanted to take a walk. He seemed uneasy about that and kept urging the taxi, but I started walking. Twenty feet from the gate, on the burning asphalt road, a boy of around thirteen came up, wearing a dark green frayed sweatshirt, shorts, and sneakers. He wanted me to follow him; he would show me Johnny Cash's house. I thanked him but said no and continued walking. A moment later he was joined by another boy, who wanted to show me a waterfall. A third boy appeared, who offered to sell me marijuana. "Best ganja on the island, right here, very cheap." He pulled a plastic bag from his shorts pocket and held it out. I told them I didn't want anything, I was just taking a walk. I was a good way from the hotel gates now, and the boys kept dancing around me, repeating their offers of Johnny Cash's house, the waterfall, and the ganja. They were not about to harm me, but nor were they about to go away anytime soon. I got rattled finally and turned back to the hotel, where the guard looked vindicated by my quick return. He shooed the boys off. "Leave the lady alone! Go home!"

The horseback ride took place the following day. The stable owner, who also acted as our guide, was dressed in a British riding costume and spoke with a British accent. After he settled our group on horses, we started off on a narrow downhill path through lush greenery (lusher and greener than the mild Catskills), then onto a broader road amid gently sloping mountains dotted by wooden shanties. Off in the distance the glassy blue-green sea glinted. Against this backdrop were herds of goats led by goatherds around five years old, women riding mules, others walking with baskets of vegetables on their heads. Groups of islanders in ragged clothes watched as we passed on our horses. One of our party waved at a small goatherd who agreed to pose for a photograph. How cute he was, the riders exclaimed, aiming their cameras, while I writhed with embarrassment.

Soon the stable owner said we had reached a village, although there was only one shoebox-shaped building in sight, made of corrugated tin, with children playing outside in the dust. The walls were spray-painted with illegible graffiti. This is a cafe, our guide said. We would stop for refreshments. We tethered the horses and filed into a dim, empty room. Farther on was a second dim room, also empty except for a bar, a refrigerator, a broken jukebox, and a young woman sitting so still it was hard to tell if she was awake or asleep, so still that in profile she resembled an African mask. She looked like the women in Matisse's paintings, only not as serene. When the guide spoke to her she reached out to open the refrigerator and took out bottles of Pepsi and Red Stripe and sullenly handed them to us.

On the way back the guide rode beside me and asked if I had seen much of the island. I told him of my attempt to take a walk the day before. "Indeed," he said. "I am so sorry. The truth is . . . I will explain it to you. They simply want to earn a few dollars, you know how it is. As a matter of fact there really is a waterfall nearby, and Johnny Cash really does have a house here. As far as the marijuana, unfortunately there are some American tourists, unfamiliar with our island, who do not know how to get their ganja from the organized, established sources."

The driver of the taxi taking us back to the hotel had to slow down almost to a stop to make way for an oncoming car, a huge white Cadillac lumbering down the dirt road, making clouds of dust rise. After it passed, "In that car," he said, "was Johnny Cash's wife."

hotels and soap

DESPITE THE PERVASIVE strain and vague guilt I felt in Jamaica, the spiffy hotel we stayed at evoked an ancient fantasy. Ever since childhood I had dreamed of hotels. I longed to stay in a real hotel with a front desk and a lobby with armchairs and carpets and potted plants and uniformed bellhops. I thought I might achieve this dream on my trip to Miami Beach with Bert and Lily—that was one of the reasons I went—but the place we stayed at was more of a rooming house or bed and breakfast affair.

Since it was not from experience, it was probably from the movies that I got the idea of what a hotel and a hotel lobby should look like. I had seen a number of the notable Catskill hotels in their heyday, but they were not what I envisioned: they were ludicrously huge and opulent and overrun by guests. I dreamed of urban hotels—four stars at least—where the management was visible and haughty and uniformed and the lobby active with guests yet serenely dignified, the kind of hotel a character in a 1940s movie would check into, where the bellboy would follow in the elevator with the bags and lead the guest to a suite, fling open the windows and unobtrusively accept a tip. Then the guest would hurriedly make an important phone call or receive a visit from a mysterious stranger, or alternatively from some thugs sent to threaten him or beat him up, and if the latter, he would awaken, dazed, send for room service and soon a wheeled tray would arrive with a bottle of champagne and a huge silver dome covering his dinner; or if he never awakened from the beating, a maid in a white ruffled apron and cap would discover his body when she came in with a pile of towels and would start to scream.

If I was careless enough to reveal my visions of glamour, my parents would laugh, as if such settings didn't exist anywhere on earth, or, on the off chance that they did, they were not for the likes of us. But they do exist, all over the place, and I would like to tell my parents, long dead, that they are not out of reach. Ordinary people stay in hotels all the time; hotels are filled with them. It is the hotel setting that makes the people in it seem other than ordinary. When I first stayed in hotels of the kind I have described, multi-starred hotels with the lobbies and elevators and so on, I felt meek and shy, as if the management were benevolently permitting me to register, and I must be on my best behavior in order to measure up to its reputation and its well-deserved stars.

I'm often in hotels or motels to give a reading or teach a class. The days are full of activities and new people. The dinners are early—hospital hours, as if the hosts want to feed you and stow you promptly away. The nights are long but not lonely. It's soothing to be alone in a room that is an abstraction of a lived-in place; it demands nothing. These are nights made for watching television, something I don't often do at home, where I lead an authentic life. It was in hotels that I discovered who Phil Donahue was and what the *Today Show* is; it's in hotels that I learn about local crime and oddments. In a St. Louis hotel I saw an unforgettable news story about a woman who opened her kitchen cabinet to discover a crouching possum. There it crouched, right on the screen: it must have waited for the cameras. Possums, I found out, are not cute as they are in children's books but can be dangerous and predatory. In this case the police came and successfully removed it.

It was in a hotel, again, an upscale hotel (maybe even five stars), that I encountered wildlife in the flesh, not on the screen. I was on a book tour, in the days when publishers were more generous with book tours, and back in my room after dinner I saw a mouse skitter out from under one of the double beds, across the carpet, and under the other bed. The hour was late and I had had a couple of drinks at dinner, so I thought perhaps I was imagining it: how could a mouse dare to infiltrate such a fancy hotel? Rodents were never part of my youthful fantasies. When I saw it again in the clear light of morning I called the front desk. Happily, this was not Orkos, where there probably was no front desk, but Boston.

A man came with a broom and dustpan and stationed himself between the beds. Though he looked mildly skeptical, he had the patience to wait, as the *Tao te Ching* advises, and the prey finally appeared. I felt vindicated as I watched the mouse-and-man scuffle. The warrior became aggressive, and while I admired his courage, I thought of the cautionary lines: "Rushing into action, you fail. Trying to grasp things, you lose them. Forcing a project to completion, you miss what was almost ripe."

In the end, the man prevailed by deftly overturning the wastebasket on top of the mouse. Just as I was wondering how I could remain in a room with a mouse under the wastebasket, a chambermaid came to lead me to another room. I went willingly and so never satisfied my curiosity about how the mouse would be transferred from under the wastebasket. Perhaps it was left there to die of starvation or suffocation.

Now that I have stayed in hotels many times, I love them, as I knew I would when I imagined them as a girl. But it took me a while to work up to the level of sophistication I craved. On our first trip as young marrieds, our guide was *Frommer's Europe on $5 a Day*. We'd saved a little money and supplemented it by borrowing three hundred dollars from my father. The places we stayed in were so cheap and correspondingly minimal—too minimal even to be rated on the one-to-five star system—that they sound mythological. In Paris we spent a month at the Hotel Henri IV (Harry says it was called the Francois I) near the Luxembourg Gardens at the rate of a dollar and a quarter a night for an attic room four flights up. You entered the shared bathroom in the hall through a concave door set in the pale-yellow wall of the narrow, winding staircase. Aside from the astonishing meagerness of the hotel—a far cry from the elegance I'd dreamed of—what I remember most about the weeks in Paris is artichokes.

Near the Henri IV was a restaurant called Chez Berthe, and it was there that we ordered our first artichokes. We didn't know what they were and chose them in a spirit of gustatory daring. When they arrived, one for each of us, sitting squat and impenetrable on their white plates, we could only stare. We might have raised our forks tentatively, but really, when you are unfamiliar with an artichoke there is no clue as to how to approach it. A kindly waitress noticed our distress and came over to help. She began plucking the leaves off and continued until she reached the straw, and finally the heart. I think of her, her shiny dark hair and rosy cheeks and ironic smile and white apron, whenever I eat an artichoke, which isn't often because I don't have the patience. I am as lazy about food as I am about travel. While I don't mind the labor of cooking, I believe that when food arrives at the table it should be ready for consumption without requiring a frontal assault, as, for instance, one must make on a lobster. The one thing I am not lazy about is writing.

In Rome, given our spare accommodations, we patronized the Albergo Diurno in the train station, where for a small sum you could rent a cubicle with a shower or bath and prepare for the day. You were given a towel and a bar of soap and a key, and there was a sliding scale of fees depending on which additional amenities you chose—shave, shampoo, manicure, and shoeshine were among the offerings—and for how long. Such places should be established in the United States, so long as we persist in doing little else for our large numbers of urban homeless people. That's not likely to happen, though. It would advertise our failure and indifference and shake our pride.

Nowadays I'm inordinately distressed—more than I like to admit—when I find myself in an aggressively ugly or shabby hotel, two stars, say. I have to resort to my fantasies about being in exile, or a potential political prisoner, and all the rest. On sleepless nights while traveling, I've given a lot of thought to that star system, trying to work out the criteria used to assign the stars.

(How I would love to serve on the rating committee, but as with other careers I dream of, like being a simultaneous translator, I have no formal qualifications.) Aside from critical features like location, size of room, furnishings, and civility of the staff, there are, or should be, other, and to me even more crucial, components: efficacy of the shower, presence of an elevator, telephone, closet and drawers (it's surprising how many hotels lack these), hair dryer, room service, and—moving into the realm of sybaritic luxury—mini-bar, chocolates left on the pillow each evening, and internet connection.

Obviously, I am way too focused on creature comforts while traveling (far more than I am at home), and that is because so little comfort of any other kind is available. Such as on a teaching gig in St. Petersburg, when our group was quartered at a dreadful and hostile hostel with flies embedded in the dust of ancient chandeliers, porcelain in the bathtub gone green like a mossy forest, rugs so frayed that your toes got caught in the strings, and some mornings, non-existent coffee, if we interpreted the waiters' grunts correctly. You might pass the front desk of this hostel a half-dozen times a day, but you still needed to show an ID card to get your key. Without it, you could be denied access to your room for hours, until the taciturn desk clerks felt you had been sufficiently chastised. Of the many comical—in hindsight—humiliations visited on us by this establishment, the most outstanding was having to request rolls of toilet paper from the slate-faced concierge who guarded supplies and generally supervised behavior: one was stationed on every floor. Learning to make the request in Russian wasn't enough. You had to prove your need by presenting— waving in her face—the empty cardboard tube of the used-up roll.

Then she might take pity. But this was Russia shortly after the fall of communism, so we were enjoined to be tolerant. I was a spoiled member of the bourgeoisie—I knew that well enough—and tried to view my deprivations as a kind of atonement, though secretly I felt no guilt whatsoever, at least not on that score.

Even more than sleek hotels, I am fond of motels. Not the shabby kind where adulterous couples meet or drug deals are consummated, though those do have their seedy charms, but the sterile, characterless Holiday Inns or Comfort Inns or Best Westerns. Their appeal is their uniformity: you know exactly what to expect. In that sense, while they lack the idiosyncratic appeal of home, such motels echo its predictability and security. They are clean (often cleaner than home), with sharp right angles (unless the TV—there's always a TV—is set triangularly in a corner to save space), and bland paintings of meadows or seascapes or horses. They all contain a laminated Room Service menu and a DO NOT DISTURB sign with PLEASE MAKE UP THIS ROOM on the other side, a message that should be superfluous. (Lately the classic imperative DO NOT DISTURB has given way to euphemism, as in PRIVACY PLEASE.) Everything else is identical: the Mr. Coffee poised complacently for use with its array of tiny accessory packets, the two glasses shrink-wrapped in plastic, the ice bucket, the white phone with its laminated instruction card, the clock-radio, the ironing board in the closet. What I dislike in the closets of cheaper motels are the hangers that won't come off the racks—presumably so guests don't steal them, an insulting imputation—but must be removed by unhooking a little metal button that fits into a groove. It's frustrating to fit these buttons back in, and for this reason I bring my own hangers, just as Harry, who likes a strong reading light, always travels with two 100-watt bulbs. The bedside lights in these motels are never adequate for reading, suggesting, depressingly, that no one reads in bed, or that hotel designers assume no one reads in bed.

Each motel bathroom has an identical hair dryer, plus miniature plastic containers of shampoo, conditioner, and hand lotion (you can judge the quality of a motel by how many of these miniature bottles they supply), paper bags for used sanitary napkins, which I glance at with nostalgia as well as satisfaction—good-bye to all that—and luxurious towels far in excess of what's needed, a fine lavishness. Anything more you require, you need only pick up the phone.

The most mysterious feature of motel rooms—if it still exists; I haven't seen it lately—is the little horizontal slit, about an inch and a half wide, in the bathroom wall above the sink and below the mirror. This is for used razor blades, a precaution, I guess, against their being left on the floor to imperil the housekeeping staff. A nice consideration: in a world of so many dangers, at least one is thoughtfully averted. But those passages behind the wall are sinister. If every room has a slit for razor blades, how many such hollow intramural columns must there be, with razors careening down, just as office and apartment buildings used to have glass-fronted mail chutes in the walls of public hallways, where people dropped outgoing letters, trustfully offering them to the force of gravity. Once in a while, waiting for an elevator, you might be startled by a stamped letter zooming past on its journey out into the world. No such public voyage awaits the used razor blades. Are they piled in heaps somewhere in the dank motel cellar? Are they ever collected, or are they abandoned, left to rust?

Maybe each bathroom has a shallow vault behind the wall that fills up and is eventually emptied by a razor-blade attendant who knows exactly where to tap the wall—Open, Sesame!—to collect the discards.

The first thing I do after checking into a motel is prowl the halls in search of the ice machine and fill the bucket, then find the soda machine and get a soda. I unpack, even if I'm only staying a day or two, and line up my things on the dresser top and in the bathroom. Then I feel right at home; after all, I've been in this room or an identical one countless times. Lately, though, it's not so easy to get into this room. Instead of a key dangling from a heavy plastic rectangle or oval, something sizable that made you feel important to be its temporary possessor, you now receive a magnetized key card. This change must be for security purposes, yet like so many measures taken for reasons of security, who ever knows if they make anyone more secure? What is known for sure is that they make things more inconvenient.

With the obsolete gigantic keys, there was always the dilemma of whether to carry them around all day or leave them at the desk, in which case you would request your key each time you came in, a humbling necessity. The cards are easier to carry, only they don't often work. You slip them in the door slot, once you happen upon the proper position of the four possible positions, and a tiny red light appears, the ubiquitous red light of modern telephones and TVs and VCRs and computers, the light that punctures the velvety darkness of bedrooms like a pinhole in the velvet. When the magnetized strip works its magic and the light turns green, the door should open by a twist of the knob. But since the green light remains on only for a split second, you have to be preternaturally swift to catch the door in its instant of potential openability. This is not easy, particularly if you are carrying a full ice bucket and a can of soda, maybe even a bag of Fritos. When after a day or two you master the timing, the magnetic strip wears out. You insert the card again and again but the green light refuses to go on. You go down to the front desk to have the card remagnetized, which the clerk does grudgingly, implying that you must have done something to render it impotent: anyone so inept at opening doors should not be allowed to leave home.

Last but far from the least of hotel amenities is soap, which really merits an essay of its own. And it has been given one, by the late writer Stanley Elkin in his collection, *Pieces of Soap*. Like me, Stanley Elkin was a collector of hotel soap. In the essay he describes his lust for hotel soap, to the point that, the first thing he would do upon checking into a hotel was not fill the ice bucket but call Housekeeping to complain, falsely, that his room had no soap. That way he got a head start on whatever he could later glean from the routine daily dispensation.

Both Stanley and I would take home as much unopened soap as we could. I do it by using the miniature bars allotted on the first day (one for the sink and a larger one for the tub) for as long as possible, down to a sliver, and saving the newer ones. I don't know where Stanley stored his soaps; I tuck them in a plastic toiletries bag under other items in case the maid should grow curious about why my soap was getting so small when she was providing two fresh bars each day. I'm aware that few if any hotel maids would interest themselves in such a matter. My suspicion comes from an intermittent, eerie sense of being watched in my most private moments (maybe this is a leftover from religious instruction, God the all-seeing), as well as a kind of narcissism—the notion that strangers are curious about the trivial details of my life. Actually it's less narcissism than projection, because—as a writer, I suppose—I am in fact curious about the trivial details of others' lives. Were I a hotel maid I very likely would speculate about the personal habits of those I cleaned up after, maybe even about how much soap they used, though I would not go so far as to rummage through their toiletries bag. I hope not, at any rate.

The soap comes in many shapes and qualities: amply or poorly sudsing, rectangular or round or oval, small or largish, though never large enough to be as solidly weighty in the hand as a real bar of soap. Its smallness gives it a provisional feeling, not quite the real thing, in keeping with the provisional nature of motels. The wrappings are white or pastel, and like many wrappings nowadays, maddeningly hard to open.

After taking home our haul of soap, Stanley and I did very different things with it. I like to use the soap; I feel I've gotten something for nothing. Also, washing with the soap reminds me of the hotel or motel, which chances are I enjoyed, because to this day staying in a hotel gives me a childish thrill, even if I might not have enjoyed or desired the trip itself.

Stanley saved the soap. I have seen the evidence. In 1996 I took a job teaching for half of each academic year at the graduate writing program of Washington University in St. Louis, where he was the stellar figure. I took the job partly because I wanted to work with him. Before the term began, on preliminary visits, we became friends. I went to his house and saw the large straw baskets—laundry baskets—filled with soap, a few on the ground floor and more upstairs. Thousands of miniature soaps. I was awed. There were more soaps than I could ever have collected even if I hadn't used them for washing. Stanley was older than I was, but that alone could not account for his greater acquisitions. He was a more fêted writer than I, so I assume he got to do more readings and visits. I wasn't envious—we were different kinds of writers and moreover he was hugely gifted and deserved every bit of his success. He deserved all his soaps too. He had earned them. It's not easy to stay in so many hotels and give so many public readings, often to small and impassive audiences. I did not begrudge him his soap. I was only mystified by his motives.

His wife, Joan, told me that Stanley so treasured his soap that once when a cleaning woman used a bar for its intended purpose he was enraged and wanted to fire her on the spot, but Joan intervened and brought him back to reason.

Harry is as attached to taking (liberating, as they used to say) hotel soaps as I, but he goes even further. If in the hallways he comes upon the maid's trolley loaded with provisions, and if the maid is not in sight, he takes soaps from the trolley—just a few, not enough to arouse suspicion, or so he thinks. In my view, maids may be perfectly aware of how many soaps they are carting around. His furtive habit bothers me. If he were apprehended, I might be prosecuted as an accomplice. For my part, I want only the soaps I am legitimately entitled to. Nevertheless, if one of us returns from a trip made alone, the first thing we ask after saying hello is, how many soaps did you get? And then we unpack and show our loot.

Our next question is not far afield—about the quality of the shower. We have never been a couple that has a lot "in common," meaning shared interests like baseball or needlework or the history of glassblowing, which used to be a prerequisite for marriage in the repressed middle of the last century, but as a result of all our travels together, we do have one common project. That is an ongoing survey of hotel and motel showers in this country and abroad, specifically, water temperature, strength of flow, height of showerhead, door vs. curtain, susceptibility to leakage. You wouldn't think so unevocative an item as a showerhead would come in so many varieties. It's cheering, in a small way, that in an era when great ingenuity is devoted to making more effective weapons and delivery systems, hundreds or possibly thousands of people are working to devise a better, or at least a different, showerhead, training their minds on the shape, density, speed and contiguity of the emerging drops.

Ce

The days before our first trip, for which I borrowed three hundred dollars from my father to stay in hotels of legendary cheapness, were frenzied because Harry had several unfinished term papers. We spent those few days in nonstop writing, rewriting and, on my part, typing. Typing was what the wives of graduate students did in those days. In high school, I had taken a one-term course in stenography and typing and became a sensational typist. Not so with stenography; all I recalled was the ubiquitous hieroglyph for "Dear Sir," a lower-case "h" with a tail at the top and the right-hand tip extending below the line. Stenography was obsolete anyway, since technology had advanced to the stage of Dictaphones. At the American Friends Service Committee in Philadelphia, where I typed away my days and got to know the personnel woman who later reappeared in my life as the wife of the director of the sanitation department in Rome (*Nettezza Urbana*), the Quaker bosses would dictate their correspondence into machines. From behind their closed doors came a steady hum, and periodically the bosses would emerge to present the secretaries with tapes. For hours on end we listened to the voices through earphones, transcribing, using a foot pedal to stop and start. Later on, during the Watergate crisis, when Richard Nixon's secretary, Rose Mary Woods, claimed that she lost eighteen minutes of a document typed from a Dictaphone, I understood exactly how that could happen, or be made to happen.

So in between packing I typed furiously, both in the sense of fast and also angry that I was typing at home as well as at the office, especially as I had recently earned a college degree from an esteemed institution. Since Harry was a graduate student and my job was negligible, we were going to Europe for the whole summer, our version of the nineteenth-century Grand Tour, when the scions of the British aristocracy set out for warm and educational continental climates. I've always wondered about those trips—the packing and laundry, that is. And where did they put a year's worth of stuff? But of course they had servants to worry about that, and to lay in their supplies of Band-aids and aspirins. Today's tourists who trail in line behind leaders holding up flags or umbrellas are the attenuated heirs of those nineteenth-century Grand Tourists. They don't stay away for a year, of course, nor are they always members of the leisure class, but their accommodations are chosen and reserved for them, their luggage is whisked off to reappear magically in their hotel rooms, their meals are provided, and their every moment accounted for. They need never encounter the dreaded void—the "What next?" which, whether at home or abroad, threatens to dismember the self and hurl its shards into an abyss.

The papers finished and handed in, we flew to London, then to Paris, then to Rome, where the great travelers of old went to be inspired and exhilarated, from which trips they would make literature: Byron, Stendhal, Goethe. To Rome, where George Eliot sent her misguided heroine, Dorothea, of *Middlemarch*, on a honeymoon with her dreadful pedant-husband, Casaubon. It is there, in "the city of visible history, where the past of a whole hemisphere seems moving in funeral procession with strange ancestral images and trophies gathered from afar," that the new bride, swathed in ingenuous idealism, begins to have doubts about her marriage. While Casaubon spends every day rooting around in the Vatican Library, Dorothea ambles through the galleries, dazed by erotic statuary she cannot begin to comprehend yet finds obscurely troubling.

We ambled through those same galleries, but I was happy to be newly married and my husband was no pedant but rather, I was discovering, the ideal traveler. Tourist, I should say. We had become tourists. Every morning we set out, Harry with the guidebook in hand, discreetly hidden but readily available. We deplored the tourists who went about brandishing their maps or guidebooks in plain view, advertising their second-class citizenship, or lack of citizenship. We began by following the plan he had outlined the night before, but it wasn't long before we deviated from it. We weren't the rigid kind of tourists. We deviated all the time, almost from the very first step. Harry was and is far more open than I to spontaneous adventure, and "walking around" remains one of his favorite occupations, at home and abroad. Walking around to see what might turn up, walking with maybe a destination in mind, a museum, a building, but nothing that couldn't be postponed if something more enticing appeared.

I followed along. I was willing to do whatever he suggested, so long as I didn't have to read the guidebook. I wasn't averse to learning about the places we visited, but reading about them beforehand was an arid task. It was all just so much information, like the facts in a textbook, which I've never been able to remember unless they're attached to something human or personal, or unless I invent a mnemonic device. I preferred to read the guidebook afterwards, when the descriptions referred to places I had already seen, heard, and smelled.

We strolled down the cobblestoned streets of Italian hill towns, streets strung with laundry just as in Italian movies, streets so narrow that if I stretched out my arms I could practically touch the facing stone walls. All the history I'd learned in school was instantly transformed from black-and-white into living color, as in the films of *The Wizard of Oz* or *The Secret Garden*. I saw many such towns and streets over the years to come, but none had the astonishing, numinous quality of that first time.

Which raises a subversive question. Of course travel is good and necessary for all sorts of reasons, but how long and how often must we do it to get the desired effect? What transformed my sense of the world on that first trip, what remains forever imprinted, I saw in an instant: that the signs were in foreign languages. That people not only spoke but lived, thought, and felt in those languages. They made love in those languages, and argued and wept and died. I saw that in each country everything, from the most banal to the most grand, was slightly different from what I had known—every sound and sight and taste registered on a different spectrum—and the ways in which things were different made for an infinitely expanding universe. But all this happened in an instant. The instantaneous and transforming quality of perception is a theme of the *Tao te Ching*. Change can come about in a blink, it counsels, provided you are ready and receptive. But after that instant—and the *Tao te Ching* does not warn of this—the rest can become work.

Tourism is a job and we were at work. (Maybe a warning sign, TOURISTS AT WORK, should be posted at historic sites, like MEN AT WORK signs near open manhole covers.) These many years later, unless a trip involves some aspect of my real work, I still see most excursions as a job: get up, get dressed, and get going. Not a job I sought, but one mysteriously assigned to me, which I mysteriously accepted. As with any job, I apply myself diligently. Except that's not the best way to be a tourist. It's far better to be Harry's kind, eager for the unexpected, ready to drop the plan at any moment. He preserves the autonomy of his real life while traveling, while I enslave myself to the job in order to get it done, the way you do with jobs you dislike and want to get over with. It's not a complicated job; it consists of walking the streets, after a while with a sort of grimness—obviously I'm not the best travel companion—and going to important places. Taking them in, consuming them. No matter what you're looking at, the nature of the job remains the same, and so it grows stale. Looking, consuming with the eye and producing nothing, can never be a genuine life.

Accordingly, locals treat tourists as people without individual identity or purpose, people who know nothing and above all are replaceable. Thousands of new ones appear each day, as reliably mass-produced as tourist trinkets. Tomorrow will bring new ones, identically ignorant and two-dimensional.

This essential sameness of tourists is not merely an ungenerous assumption on the part of those who must endure them. Tourists do tend to melt down and merge, as it were, to assimilate, until whatever uniqueness they possessed gets ground down to a common pulp, like vegetables in a blender. During our most recent trip, the one I nearly aborted by leaving my passport at home, I found fresh evidence of this, on a bus lumbering through Sicily. Harry and I listened, unavoidably, to the conversation of an American couple seated behind us.

"We'll have to find the bus to Siracusa when we get there."

"They did say there was a connecting bus, didn't they?"

"Yes. At least I think that's what they said. There must be."

"Well I hope it's in the same station and not at the other end of town."

"They said it was. If not we'll just get a taxi to the right station. There are always plenty of taxis around bus stations."

"There are?"

"Well, I would imagine. Don't you think?"

The disturbing thing about this banal conversation was that we had just had an identical one ourselves. In its many permutations, it is the classic tourist conversation; one can spend a goodly portion of each day on just this sort of dialogue.

In the process of changing buses we struck up an acquaintance with this couple, our uncanny doppelganger, and Harry, who is impulsively friendly, suggested we have dinner together one night, since we were headed for the same touristy neighborhood.

These impromptu connections are iffy, usually inspired more by loneliness and boredom than genuine affinity. Sometimes, it is true, especially if one is traveling alone, they can lead to re-vivifying love affairs, as they apparently did for the Victorian Englishwomen, but apart from the fact that we were traveling in pairs, I could tell right off that no such eruption would come of our dinner date with Tom and Maggie. Before the date I predicted that Tom would turn out to be a dentist and Harry surmised that this was not a first marriage for either of them. At dinner, a pro-tracted affair at which we learned that they owned two Porsches and played a lot of golf, it turned out that Harry was right. As far as the dentist part, not quite: Tom was a retired lawyer but Maggie's first husband had been a dentist, so I considered myself not altogether mistaken.

The job of tourist is made more laborious by ignorance: you don't know where anything is or how anything works. In this it re-sembles starting any new job. Those first few stressful days, often strewn with minor humiliations, you're clueless as an infant and must depend on the kindness of strangers for the most basic infor-mation, as I did at Popular Science Publishing Company (though strangers are as a rule more helpful than the loathsome Mary F.). You don't know which bus to take and where to put the fare or the ticket, or what the items on the menu mean, or how to read the train schedule, or what hours the museums are closed (in Italy at whimsical times).

Dedicated travelers claim that learning a new country's trivia is part of the delight of travel. I can grant that. Writers operate the same way, amassing small bits of data to build a large visionary structure. The daily mores and methods of any culture are intriguing in themselves, and there is an element of theatrical pleasure, as well, in aping or adopting the ways of others. I am ready to learn to be a Roman in Rome. It's that primal state of ignorance that engenders a low-level slow-burning panic, leaving its ashy residue even after I've mastered the bus schedules and the route back to the hotel.

If only someone, my elusive twin or the double I've always dreamed of having, could make the first trip for me. Let *her* get through all that initial fumbling. Then on the next visit, incorporating her smattering of familiarity, I might manage to enjoy myself. In fact, this longing to have someone live through a first encounter or experience for me goes not merely for travel but for many critical life experiences that improve as they progress or recur: first day of school, first real sex, childbirth, as well as certain intimate medical procedures so sadistic that they strain credibility but one submits to, perforce. Surely each of us has our own list.

Above all, the longing applies to writing. I yearn for an accommodating double to provide my first drafts. Afterwards, I'd be more than happy to rewrite as much and as often as necessary. But facing the quivering mass of unsorted stuff in the mind is even worse than finding the right bus in St. Petersburg. I especially longed for this gifted double when I was teaching in southern California and again attempting a mystery novel—progeny of my unfulfilled novel begun in the seventh grade—again rather melodramatic and again about identical twins. One dies and one lives on, forever missing her sister. Even without a double, I managed to write a good bit of it, but again never finished. I couldn't work out the plot, but even more, I couldn't work out what it all

meant, what it was *for*. The story was a series of calamities befall-
ing a family, but it had no underlying purpose. I think I simply
enjoyed heaping tragedy at the doorstep of this unfortunate family out of a masochistic anger and resentment that I had agreed
to teach in southern California, alone and alienated. Evenings I
would eat dinner in front of the TV news. It was 1991. I watched
the Gulf War—missiles exploding in air like a fireworks display,
the commentators insanely gleeful about the new technology—and
I watched the Los Angeles police beating Rodney King with their
clubs, a scene shown every evening for weeks. After dinner and
the war and the beating, I read. My stint in Southern California
was ten weeks, so I was reading the longest novel I could find,
Alessandro Manzoni's *The Betrothed*, which vividly depicted
the fourteenth-century plague. Decaying, pustulating bodies lay
crammed together in smelly shelters, while two forcibly separated
lovers searched for each other. No wonder I took out my frustration on that poor family I invented.

For years after, I carried those melodramatic pages about
the twins—one doomed in adolescence, the other doomed to live
bereft—wherever I went, but wasn't able to make anything coherent out of them.

(℘)

I always felt a bit guilty, on our first trip, that I didn't sufficiently
appreciate the privilege of visiting places my friends back in
Brooklyn were still dreaming about. Just recently I came upon a
validation of my feelings from no less than Matisse himself. Amélie,
Matisse's wife, told Gertrude Stein about the couple's first trip to

Italy in 1907, a fulfillment of Amélie's childhood dream, and Stein reported her words in *The Autobiography of Alice B. Toklas*: "I say to myself all the time, I am in Italy. And I say it to Henri all the time and he is very sweet about it, but he says, what of it."

What of it, indeed? How refreshing to find that a great artist shared my feelings and was willing to say so, at least to his wife. Reticent as Matisse was, he might not have spoken so freely had he known he would be quoted in print. Over and above the "what of it?" attitude, Matisse was irritated, on that Italian trip, by the overzealous attention of his host, Leo Stein, the art collector and brother of Gertrude, who shepherded him relentlessly around the Uffizi Galleries in Florence, soliciting his opinions of the paintings. Matisse's frustration must have been apparent, and off-putting. After that trip Leo Stein, who had been one of his chief collectors, never bought another Matisse work.

Apart from this trip, Matisse was an indefatigable traveler, taking off whenever he needed refreshment, which was constantly. Travel, he said, "was a means of cleansing the eye." He and Amélie spent their honeymoon trip in London, to see the Turners at the National Gallery. Later on, in quest of new varieties of light, a light that would release him from the gray lowering skies of his northern childhood, he spent summers in the south of France, especially Collioure, on the Mediterranean coast, the part of France closest to Africa. The thought of the Matisses packing up their household, their three small children, and the painting supplies several times a year to go south is oppressive. No wonder Amélie eventually collapsed and spent years barely leaving her bed. It wasn't only Matisse's difficult and demanding temperament that laid her low. It was that ceaseless packing.

By the time he settled in Nice, around 1920, Matisse also owned a large house in a northern suburb of Paris. He shuttled back and forth between the two, sometimes with and sometimes without the long-suffering Amélie and the rest of his entourage. He went farther afield, too, to Corsica, to Spain, where he was deathly ill, to Algeria, Morocco, Germany, and Russia, to be dazzled by the medieval religious icons. In the United States he was "electrified" by New York City, where the light was "so dry, so crystalline, like no other." In his sixties he visited Tahiti: there the light was "like plunging your eye into a golden goblet."

Despite all this movement, the "what of it" attitude remained. He traveled "in order to see his inner landscape in a fresh light," his biographer, Hilary Spurling, writes. "Exotic settings meant nothing to him." His traveling became part of the weave of his life, as necessary and integral as the fabrics he collected and hung in his studio, recalling his youth in a town of weavers.

After our trip, the three hundred dollar debt to my father preyed on my mind. I didn't like owing him money although he never mentioned it and probably never would have, had we failed to return it. Still, it nagged at me. This was before credit cards made owing money a respectable, even patriotic, way of life, before citizens became consumers, subway passengers became customers, and therapists' patients, clients. Within a few months after our return I had saved up three hundred dollars. I hastily wrote a check and popped it in an envelope. I was light-hearted, unburdened of my debt. When my father received the check he called to say how ungracious my gesture was—putting the check in an envelope without even a brief note attached. This was a very unusual thing for my father to do. He rarely commented on nuances of behavior; rather, when he was displeased, he would shout wildly. But this he said in a quiet, dejected tone, more in sorrow than in anger. I was mortified. I grasped how crude I had been. I had hurt his feelings, returning his loan as if I were paying a bill to the phone company. One tends to think that brash, angry people do not have feelings to be hurt, but I learned otherwise. I have never again sent anyone anything businesslike without some personal words attached.

Soon after my father died (years after I so boorishly repaid the three hundred dollars), I took to dropping in on my Aunt Lily and Uncle Bert, who had initiated me into the wonders and perils of travel on that first trip to Miami Beach. They had moved from Brooklyn to midtown Manhattan, a high-rise apartment building from which Bert, in his retirement, roamed the city. Once I met him on the subway, on his way to a Russian class downtown. I didn't know how much Russian he remembered from his childhood, if any, or how much he had had to begin with. The family originally came from a town near Kiev, though I never heard a word of Russian spoken by my father, my grandparents, or my seven aunts and uncles. They probably spoke Yiddish growing up, but they must have known some Russian. Unlike Bert, my father wished to delete that segment of his life altogether. After his death, going through his papers, I found an old report card in Russian, listing his subjects and grades. I could read the Cyrillic alphabet and had taught myself a bit of the language: from that bit I made out what the subjects were—geometry, grammar, geography—and it appeared that his grades were excellent.

I would go over to Bert and Lily's in the late afternoon and be given tea or a drink. Then I would look at Bert and listen to him talk—about his travels, his past, his law practice, politics. It didn't matter what. I just liked to look and listen. I felt slightly hypocritical about the visits, since their main reason was that I missed my father, and Bert looked and sounded so much like him. Were I from California I might say his "aura" was similar. Bert was short and slight—my father was stockier—and his manner was more curt, and he had less white hair (family rumor claimed that Bert, in his vanity, had had hair implants, but if so they hadn't helped much). Still, the resemblance was strong, especially the voice and the inflections and the elegant fluency. I would have liked to close my eyes and simply hear his voice, but of course that would never do. Sometimes I brought my children along.

My father was not the only person Bert resembled. Back in the 1960s when the name of Ariel Sharon, then a general in the Israeli Army, began to appear in news reports, it occurred to me that perhaps he was a relative. Sharon was my family name as well, shortened and Anglicized when the family emigrated before World War I. I'd heard that the general's family was from Russia too. If we were related, I fantasized, I could go to Israel and look him up. What a lark, to be entertained by a general, surely the only time such an opportunity would come my way, given my distinctly unmilitary connections.

I began asking my old aunts and uncles about Ariel Sharon, those remaining of the eight who had emigrated here. A ninth, the oldest brother, had remained in or near Kiev because he was already married and embarked on an adult life. Unless he got out before the war, in all likelihood he was a victim of the Nazi massacre at Babi Yar and thrown into the ditch with so many others. Once I asked my father what had become of him. It was touchy to approach my father on this subject because he pretended those first twelve years of his life did not exist, so I asked very tentatively. He didn't know, he said, only at some point the family stopped receiving letters.

There were two schools of thought on the subject of Ariel Sharon. My Aunt Frieda, a preternaturally shrewd, skinny, angular woman with a stiletto-like tongue—the female version of the family's vehemence—definitely believed him to be one of us. From earliest childhood I'd trusted her intelligence and instincts. Others were not so sure. Bert, who had fixed opinions about everything, was for once uncertain. I didn't know how to pursue the matter, by way of research, that is. At that time there were no biographies of Sharon that I knew of, and no Google. Anyhow, I am a poor researcher and have always preferred fantasy, where everything is possible, over fact, where a single explanation shackles the imagination.

I did go so far as to look him up in an encyclopedia. What I found was not promising. His family did come from Russia, but they had emigrated to Israel long before my branch left. The other facts I've forgotten, except that they didn't fit either.

Standing in opposition to the facts was the matter of temperament. Over the years that I dithered on and off with the notion of possible kinship, every exploit of Ariel Sharon's seemed to be generated from the same DNA that had produced my father, my uncles and aunts, my cousins. Me. He was willful, quick to anger, heedless of caution, a juggernaut when it came to pursuing his goals. He shocked people, first by his rashness and bravery and later by his single-minded ruthlessness. This was all very familiar, even if on a grander scale than I was accustomed to. At the time of his 1982 foray into the refugee camp in Lebanon I was at the point of hoping he was not a blood relation. "Weapons are the tools of fear," says the *Tao te Ching*,

> a decent man will avoid them
> except in the direst necessity
> and, if compelled, will use them
> only with the utmost restraint. . . .
> His enemies are not demons,
> but human beings like himself.

Watching Sharon's career, I was thankful that my father and his brothers and sisters had never been in a position of political or military power. Whatever damage they had done had at least been in the domestic sphere.

But the resemblance to Bert: after I'd stopped thinking about the matter, indeed avoided it, my mother showed me a photograph of Ariel Sharon in *Time* magazine. "You were wondering if he was a relative," she said. "Just look at this. He's a fat Bert." She was right. A fat Bert. A Bert blown up with air and stuffed into a uniform. The resemblance was uncanny. I hoped it was coincidental. Sometimes old people, particularly those from the same ethnic background, start to look alike.

Bert—the thin Bert, who definitely was in the family—appreciated my visits and sometimes gave me small gifts, once a silver dollar he said was very valuable ("You of course don't know anything about coins but believe me, take it to a professional and you'll see, it's worth a lot") or trinkets from his various travels, the kinds of things one might give to children. Because he appreciated my visits, he promised that he would take Harry and me along on his next trip, which was to be a cruise down the Amazon, at some vague future date. Harry and I developed a running joke about this hypothetical cruise down the Amazon, envisioning ourselves lounging on deck chairs with a lot of rich old people, hearing the lapping of the murky water and watching the jungle drift past. My visions were conjured from Conrad's *Heart of Darkness,* even though that was another continent and another century. Still, we looked forward to it, out of curiosity. So we were dismayed, a few years later—by then my visits to Bert and Lily had grown less frequent—to learn that they had already cruised down the Amazon without us.

no movement

AT THE AGE OF twenty-four the British critic Cyril Connolly complained of "a horror of being stationary, a panic fear of keeping still," which drove him back and forth across the English Channel every few months. One might, mistakenly, attribute his perpetual motion to youthful restlessness or to talent not yet certain of its contours. But age has nothing whatsoever to do with it.

Connolly's affliction is a fear of the void, of what is—or rather what is not—inside us. I suspect that some form of his "panic fear," though not always so intense, is what impels frequent flyers. It's a fear that imitates hunger, and sends us through the airport's surveillance barriers as if they were the gateway to satiety—or at least relief from panic or boredom, two shadows cast by the same penumbral shape.

As everyone knows, air travel in itself not only fails to relieve panic or boredom but can exacerbate them. It certainly does for me, although things have improved since my seatmate on a flight to Chicago, a chatty pilot, told me about her flying lessons. When I asked if she'd been scared at the beginning, she said with a chuckle, What for? It's not going to drop out of the sky. Why not? I asked. That was precisely what I'd always wondered. She proceeded to explain the principles of aerodynamics, using the analogy of ships floating on water, and for a few minutes I understood why planes do not drop out of the sky. I no longer remember the science, but knowing that I did once grasp those principles for five minutes still sustains me when I board a plane.

According to environmentalists, air travel is one of the primary and most intractable causes of global warming. An article in *The Nation* in May of 2007 describes in fairly terrifying terms the enormous damage done to the environment by "lifting a large passenger plane into the air and keeping it there." The author, George Monbiot, considers all the possible alternatives to fossil fuel—biofuels such as oil palm, sugarcane, and soybeans, or hydrogen made from renewable electricity—only to find each of them in some way impractical or pernicious. He goes on to reject alternative modes of transport like passenger ships and ultra-high-speed trains, again on the grounds of environmental damage or prohibitive inefficiency. The only mode of travel he can conscientiously recommend is the zeppelin or blimp (of Hindenburg notoriety, though Monbiot assures us that blimps are now quite safe). But, he admits ruefully, "A flight from New York to London by airship would take forty-three hours." Given American habits and tastes, that is not likely to be a popular choice any time soon. Besides, after forty-three hours aloft, the passengers' panic and boredom might have grown to such chronic proportions that they might not recede even at the sight of Big Ben or the Tower of London. In the end, the only solution Monbiot sees for the future of the planet is less air travel.

That would be fine with me, but I'm in a minority. Preferring to stay put is practically disreputable in a cultural climate that prizes mobility, haste, multitasking and optimum consumption of sights, sounds, and experiences. An economy rooted in the culture of greed must place a premium on consuming rather than producing anything, even experience. Gerhard Schulze, a German sociologist, has a word for "a society obsessed by the need to have numerous experiences": *Erlebnisgesellschaft*. His analogy for this form of consumption is, not surprisingly, the marketplace, "where experiences become commodities but also wear out, producing a constant demand for escalation towards a more eventful life."

To keep the whole machinery running and growing, we need to consume other cultures at the great mall of travel, and we grow bloated on them. Even our military and imperial exploits contribute to the consumption stampede. The easiest aspect of a culture to appropriate or imitate is cuisine. After the Vietnam War, Vietnamese restaurants sprang up everywhere, not only in regions where Vietnamese people settled. Beyond new foods, our wars generate an educational by-product: they set us to studying the history, the customs, the music, of the places we've bombed. Since the September 11 attacks and the retaliatory wars in Afghanistan and Iraq, we have been flooded by books and analyses of Middle Eastern history and religion, not to mention music and theater. This is all salutary, certainly. But it is also salutary to remember that it was violence that propelled them into our line of vision.

I came across Schulze's prodigious word in *On Holiday: A History of Vacationing*, by the Swedish anthropologist, Olvar Lofgren. "*Erlebnisgesellschaft*," Lofgren explains,

> has the same root as the Swedish "*upplevelse*" and translates roughly into "living through something," an event that turns experience into an experience, something uplifting and out of the ordinary—something with an end and a beginning and thus also articulated and transformed into expression.

Clearly this kind of inflated experience, and not the common sort connoted by our paler English word, is what travelers are seeking. What we're all seeking, whether at home or abroad or in between, waiting in line at the airport, shoeless.

Lofgren's subject, treated in droll fashion, is not so much traveling, really, as vacationing—mountains, beaches, spas. That is, release from the daily tedium rather than any hankering for new experiences or self-improvement, still less Camus' sober confrontation with the self. He traces the origins of tourism and its attendant industry, starting with the eighteenth-century Europeans who discovered that nature might be a source of delight and revitalization, as opposed to the prevailing agricultural view. Their discovery produced the notion of the picturesque, which gave us, in turn, the picture postcard and tourist photography, right up to today's Camcorder. The picturesque, as apprehended in England and applied to the English garden, included some quaint features.

> The cottage or hermit's cave was a standard element in the English garden. . . . More ambitious garden projects tried to supply real hermits. In 1791 a Swedish newspaper mused over the attempt of a British gentleman to recruit

a live hermit. Applicants were required to endure seven years in total silence in the hermitage of the garden, to wear sandals and simple dress, not to cut their hair or nails, to drink water from the babbling brook, and to sit with a Bible, some optical elements, and an hourglass in view of visitors. The remuneration for these seven years would be 700 guineas, but alas the chosen applicant endured only three weeks.

Perhaps the hermit might have lasted longer had he studied the *Tao te Ching* on the subject of non-doing:

> Do you have the patience to wait
> till your mud settles and the water is clear?
> Can you remain unmoving
> till the right action arises by itself?

Or, as Arthur Waley puts it, in an unexpected access of poetry,

> Which of you can assume such murkiness, to become in the
> end still and clear?
> Which of you can make yourself inert, to become in the end
> full of life and stir?

Hermits aside, any attempt to produce rather than consume experience, to be our own supplier rather than shop in the global marketplace, fostering the spiritual inflation of *Erlebnisgesellschaft*, requires a degree of stillness. If we make ourselves inert, meaning do nothing by force of will, things will start to happen on their own. To ferment and rise. Productive action will generate itself out of what we've accumulated and stored. Ideally, thought will arise—and thought is action too.

But only if we turn off the electronic beeping whose goal is to circumvent thought, to render thought and its rigors obsolete. Instead of thought, technology offers information. (IT makes it happen, an ad promises.) It also offers the illusion of perpetual connection, engagement, community. But a Blackberry can no more fill an existential void than compulsive eating or gambling can relieve angst for any more than a few minutes. In April of 2007 when the Blackberry system shut down for about twelve hours, an epidemic of panic struck its users. Psychiatrists, our first responders, rushed in with analyses. *The New York Times*, in typical fashion announcing trends months after they've peaked, reported the doctors' findings. "Social needs and yearnings may drive the use. But at some point that use becomes an end unto itself, a physical ritual that can take on some of the qualities of actual addiction." Dr. John Ratey, a Harvard professor, coined the phrase "acquired attention deficit disorder" for "people who are accustomed to a constant stream of digital stimulation and feel bored without it."

For the Blackberry addicts, as with those who travel constantly for diversion, the present moment—where they are in time and space and in their own lives—is simply not good enough. Not enough to relieve the ennui of being alive, the boredom/panic reaction when nothing is happening.

The notion that salvation can come through information, let alone that IT can make anything happen, is a delusion. Without accompanying thought, information flickers, deadly, on the computer screen, like the reflexive processes of a body on life support while the brain is dead. The information age (or age of too-much-information, known colloquially as TMI), has conned us into thinking that the possession of facts has merit or power in its own right. Facts are needed, certainly. But very little can be accomplished without a mind to juggle and order the facts, to calibrate their rhythms and relations, make them loop and twirl in the air, and come to rest in the hand. There is no way of circumventing the use of the mind, which requires being where we are.

Nonetheless, when we're gripped by uncertainty, travel feels like a ready solution to the problem of What next? What to do, what to think, what to be? (Time was when cigarettes were ideal for those moments, but now that relief has been taken from us.) On a trip, there's always another monument, another excursion, another natural wonder to visit, to prove to ourselves that we're doing something.

What would happen if we refused to flee and stayed home instead? The initial void, what we travel to escape, might be terrifying. What if we peered right in? We've all approached the edge many times. We step back gingerly and hurry to find something to do next, before we're fully aware of being so close to falling. Retreat becomes automatic, habitual. We do errands or we work, we reach for a book or the phone or the remote. But sometimes the abyss sneaks up on us, or we on it, and we're on the cliff edge of emptiness, no firm ground beyond. It might happen while we're heading down the street and suddenly lose sight of what was our errand, or come to the end of some rote action, unloading the dishwasher, say, or are in between things—hanging up the phone and forgetting what its ringing interrupted. What can we go back to? What was supposed to be next? Panic surges in. What will happen in the next five minutes? The next five years? What will we think about? What is there to think about? Those are moments when the threads that bind us to the particulars of our lives fall from our grasp; the self is in eclipse, leaving us no more than a solitary consciousness casting about for something to be conscious of. Those are the moments when we start planning a trip.

Although, as my waking in the dark in Orkos, in the middle of the Aegean sea, illustrates, those moments can occur on a trip as well, bringing even more dread: there's nowhere to go—we're already there. That vast emptiness (what William James called a sense of "vastation") can be even more suffocating away from home. It may be kin to the state Camus was referring to, "feverish but also porous." "We come across a cascade of light, and there is eternity." In Orkos, on the contrary, eternity visited in a cascade of darkness.

These recurrent voids, whether at home or abroad, are not even the big one—the certainty of death on its way, maybe not far off. They are only the small intimations (or imitations) of it, like potholes a car might fall into, compared to an Alpine crevasse. We all design our own modes of distraction from the knowledge of mortality, or our modes of confrontation. But as for the smaller voids, instead of logging onto some travel website, it's possible to wait them out. We teeter on the edge, maybe with a mild vertigo. We might feel a sneaky urge to let go and topple in, but being sane, we put up a sensible resistance. None of this is pleasant. But if we can endure it, something will turn up, something banal that restores us to our lives. Once again the threads reappear in our hands, tethering us to our circumstances. We can breathe freely. We know who we are. We were only lost for a moment. True, we suspect that we are still lost, have always been lost and always will be. But being lost becomes more tolerable when we know we'll soon recover the illusion of being found. Maybe madness is the state of being forever lost in the intolerable truth, without the capacity—whether that capacity is a strength or a weakness—to be distracted from it.

In his book about vacationing, Lofgren writes that early travelers found nothing particularly beautiful about the seashore, in fact considered it barren and "not even picturesque." Visitors to the early spas built near the sea went for health—the salt air—not for beauty or a hint of infinity. Things have evolved since then. Beach culture is elaborate, with endless accoutrements needed to set up an encampment. Besides blankets, towels, sunscreen, and all the rest, different beaches have different practices arising more or less organically from the landscape or the ethos of its inhabitants. Just as Caribbean beaches have their thatched huts, Greek island beaches have their geometric grids of chairs and umbrellas set out parallel to the shoreline (after Euclid, presumably), for which you pay a small fee and receive a written receipt from an attendant who prowls the territory the way ice-cream vendors used to prowl the Coney Island beaches with freezer boxes dangling from their necks like giant pendants. Likewise, German beaches have an un-usual custom noted in *On Holiday*; the description could only be diluted by paraphrase:

> On some German beaches you may spot a sign telling you that it is absolutely forbidden to build sand castles. This

may, to an outside visitor, seem like a harsh attitude to a harmless occupation, but then you have probably not seen what a German sand castle may look like. We are not talking about miniatures here but the old tradition of building a secluded, circular wall around your beach territory, to protect yourself from the wind and the regards of others. . . . On a real German sand castle beach you may have to maneuver your way past castle after castle, and then it might also feel like walking through an art show, because the German tradition puts great emphasis on decoration. . . .

The tradition of placing yourself inside a sand castle was well established in the nineteenth century. It probably started as a way of claiming space on the beach and also as a protection against the often chilly winds of German beaches. The tradition soon triggered off competition and the idea of building a more perfect and more beautiful structure around yourself. Some of the structures had elegant patterns accomplished with shells or wreckage, and many had sand sculptures.

. . . The nastier ones are some of the sand castles from the 1930s, as the one with Hitler's portrait in sand and the title 'Unser Fuhrer.' This sand castle is photographed surrounded with happy beachgoers in swimwear doing the Heil Hitler salute.

. . . . When German tourists after the Second World War started traveling abroad they brought along their building tradition, not always aware of the kind of signals they were sending. In countries like Holland and Denmark, where the same beaches had been occupied by Nazi troops, surprised Germans found their castles trampled down when they returned to the beach next morning. Local youths had demolished them during the night.

An earlier source of conflicts was the tradition of putting up flags on the beach. This was a late nineteenth-century tradition, found not only in Germany, but travelers from this young nation often took along flags when they went abroad. The tradition led to international conflicts, as locals saw it as a symbol of aggressive Germanness, the quest for Lebensraum. On one of the beaches in Denmark where there were many German castles and flags, local Danes went out and removed the flags. German tourists protested, and in the end the two governments had to exchange stern notes.

In Jamaica, I would get out to the beach very early. The only others around were the uniformed guard and several men raking the sand, removing all imperfections before the tourists appeared. The guard would greet me. "Do you like our island so far? The sun shines ninety percent of the time." After we chatted, I would select a thatched hut. The beach was lined with those huts—big umbrellas, really—about eight feet apart. Each morning you fetched a beach chair and towel, and staked your claim to a hut by placing the chair squarely in front, the towel draped over it. This quickly became a ritual, like the urban rituals of reserving a seat in the movies, or finding one on the subway. Then you would repair to the terrace for the buffet breakfast, an abundance of pastel-colored tropical fruits.

After breakfast, as people settled into their chairs beside the huts, music was piped onto the beach from a public address system: a brass band playing Harry Belafonte's "Day-O": "Come mister tally man tally me banana." The morning after my horseback ride and encounter with Johnny Cash's car, I lay on my chair examining my fellow tourists. A man in the hut to the right, with a mustache and mutton-chop sideburns, caught my eye because of his grotesque shape, an enormous belly hanging over his bathing trunks, supported by short, thick legs and small feet in rubber sandals. In the hut to the left was an American couple with six children. Every few minutes they called: "Adam! Eric! Mark! Lisa! Keith! Heather! Not so far out! Stay inside the ropes! Ride the waves, Adam!" Two of the older children rented a Jet Ski, which galloped over the aqua waters making a stupendous noise.

Suddenly the Harry Belafonte song on the loudspeaker was interrupted by a woman's piercing voice: "Ladies and gentlemen, we are about to begin our daily crab races in the pool area. Please come to the pool area to place your bets. Remember, we cannot change bills over twenty dollars U.S., we do not have the money. All change will be given in local currency. Come and have a look at the crabs in their crate before you place your bets. You will see the crate is covered with glass so you have nothing to fear. Nothing at all to fear. Please look the crabs over and decide which crab you think will get out of the chalk circle first."

Crab races? Well, why not? Vacations are for silliness. I joined the crowd going towards the pool. In their glass-covered crate, the crabs slogged about morosely on their bellies. Their shells were painted different colors: red, orange, yellow, blue, green. "Ladies and gentlemen," said the woman, whom I could now see, a tall, elegant fortyish woman wearing a silk print dress and high-heeled shoes, looking anomalous among the half-naked tourists. She stood at the deep end of the pool holding a microphone. "I want to warn you about one thing: these crabs are very shy and nervous. The slightest movement may upset them. When we let them out to begin the race, you may make as much noise as you like with your cheering and so on, you may tear the place apart with your voices, but no movement, please. Okay, we are almost ready to take the crabs out of the crate now. Place your bets. The odds are, red—ten to one; orange—eight to one; green—six to one; blue—four to one; yellow—two to one. And here they go! Remember, no movement! These crabs are shy and nervous. Easily startled."

The crabs moved with excruciating slowness, and not always in the direction of their goal, out of the chalk circle. They didn't know money was riding on them. Unlike racehorses, they didn't even know they were competing, that they had a goal. The tourists of every nationality whooped and cheered—Olé! Bravo!—but obediently made no movement. The woman announced their progress: "Red is off to a good start with green close behind, followed by orange and yellow. Blue has not yet begun to move. Green is gradually taking the lead, yes, green has overtaken red, now blue is moving, coming up behind yellow, orange a close second now that red has turned back. Blue is making a dash forward—"

All at once a tourist, the fat man from the beach, reached out and snatched the crab painted red. He held him high up and roared in a German accent, "Move, you son of a bitch!" Everyone gasped.

"No movement, please!" the woman at the microphone implored. "Please, sir, put the crab down." The man shook the crab. His face was very red; it was hard to tell if he was joking or really angry at the crab. All at once he gave a shriek, dropped the crab, and clutched his wrist. As the crab shattered on the ground, blue and green and yellow slime seeping from its broken shell, a stream of blood oozed from the man's wrist.

"The goddamn thing bit me!" he yelled. Attendants from the bar rushed up with cocktail napkins, dabbed at the man's wrist and wrapped it up, then led him off, sputtering, towards the main building.

"We're very sorry for the disturbance, ladies and gentleman," said the elegant woman, restored to calm. "We warned you about the crabs. They are very easily upset. Ordinarily they are as gentle as sheep, but they do not like to be disturbed. Now we will continue with the race. Blue has passed yellow and is coming up behind orange. . . ."

I left the crab races and returned to my room to lie down. Yet again, I wondered why I was here and why I had ever left home, where I wouldn't have had to think about things like crab races. My mother's self-imposed, safe narrowness began working its old seduction.

Quite by accident, I came upon my mother after her death, resuscitated in two dimensions. I was returning to New York City from Washington, D.C., when on the train I ran into a woman I'd gone to college with, who had become a librarian at the Library of Congress. I can't remember what conversational byway led us to the Catskills, but she revealed that her family had owned the Hotel Nemerson, where she spent a good part of her childhood. The Nemerson was a household name among aficionados of the Catskills in their glory years. My companion told me of a documentary film about the Catskills: *The Rise and Fall of the Borscht Belt.*

Given my feelings about the Catskills, this was hardly an item I would go out and search for, only she said it contained scenes of the amateur entertainments staged in the various hotels and bungalow colonies. That meant I had to find it. It might show my mother, who had been dead for about twelve years. If there was a chance to see her in action again, I didn't want to miss it. An enthusiastic amateur torch singer with a vast reportoire, at parties my mother would break into one of her signature numbers— "Diamonds Are a Girl's Best Friend" was one—at the slightest encouragement. She could sing her sexy cabaret songs so that every man in the room felt she was singing to him alone in the dark. And yet her performance was made ambiguous by a quality I can only call "wholesome." Wholesomeness, when I was old enough to discern and understand it, to my mind wiped out, like a coat of spanking white paint on a grainy old wall, most of what made life interesting—the gradual accumulation of flaws and dirt. Her sunny glow suggested that she both meant and didn't mean the words and gestures of the songs. This is how I'd seduce you if I wanted to, but of course I wouldn't dream of it. It's all just good clean fun. A kind of peek-a-boo, teasing quality.

The combination of sexiness and wholesomeness, in addition to talent, made her the unchallenged star of the musical reviews produced every summer at our bungalow colony. These were written by a schoolteacher, the only husband whose work allowed him to be in residence all summer. He must have spent a good part of the winter thinking up the skits spoofing Catskills life and concocting the lyrics set to popular tunes, for which he drafted the corps of willing women and led them through weeks of painstaking rehearsal. Somewhere in a desk drawer I have crumbling copies of these lyrics on the crinkly onionskin paper once used for carbon copies. Even now I sometimes find myself silently singing them in my head.

In these shows my mother found her métier. Sumptuous Brown's Hotel, a few miles down the road, might boast of Jerry Lewis and Sid Caesar, but we had my mother and her chorus line of housewives. Children were generally not admitted to this late Saturday-night event—the shows were spiced with off-color jokes that today would not make a ten-year-old blink—but I had special privileges because my mother was the main feature. I even attended the afternoon rehearsals (scheduled between games of bridge and mah-jongg), where I was occasionally enlisted to play the piano for the cast, whose children were in the pool or necking in the woods. On opening night, the only night, as I watched my mother cavort onstage I felt a potent blend of secret pride and squirming embarrassment. Only later did I realize how talented she was—she deserved better than the makeshift stage of our casino. Indeed, she sometimes wished regretfully that she had pursued a singing career, but she never came right out and said why she hadn't. Fear, surely. Fear of leaving the cozy, safe, wide circle of family and friends where she was the luminescent, admired center, and venturing out into the larger world. There she might encounter strangeness and would be gripped by what Camus calls "the instinctive desire to go back to the protection of old habits."

To my surprise, I found the film in a branch of the New York Public Library, which immediately lent it dignity. It was fifty-two minutes long. I watched, tense with anticipation; I had a premonition that she would appear. Past the halfway mark, the actor Joseph Wiseman, who was narrating, mentioned the name of our bungalow colony in his mellifluous tones. The owner's son, once young and dashing, flashed on the screen, middle-aged and bearded. I held my breath. There she was, in her black satin, sequined dress and white fez, twirling her silver cane, having a fantastic time. My mother, who was so leery of foreign parts, had no fear whatsoever of strutting and swaggering across the stage in her home territory, leading a chorus line of chunky women in modified Can-can ruffled outfits, before an audience of two hundred.

She was onscreen for about thirty seconds. I replayed those thirty seconds half a dozen times. I bought the video and showed it to my sister and brother, who didn't seem as excited by it as I was. I showed it to my children. I tried to locate the original tapes so I could see more of her, but with no luck. It seems the old tapes—along with still photos of my mother that used to hang in the casino—are in a collection of cartons somewhere in the library of the University of Indiana at Bloomington, not yet archived. The librarian I spoke to said I could come to Bloomington if I liked and go through the cartons.

Now and then I watch the video. Each time I see her, at the peak of her performance, I feel like jumping up and shouting, "Yes!," with a high five sign of triumph, which *101 American Customs* describes as

> a pervasive gesture in American culture that indicates enthusiastic approval and acceptance of a deed or incident. This gesture may have sprung from the old Roman gesture of raising the right arm in praise or tribute to the emperor.

In post-imperial Rome during the Fulbright year that had my mother so worried about our welfare, Harry and I had plans to go out for dinner on November 22. Three friends were coming to our apartment for a drink first—an Italian translator who'd been our teacher in Perugia at the Università per Stranieri's three-week crash course in Italian; her husband, who was an American writer; and another Fulbright, an older man, we thought, though he was in his early forties, graying, balding, and cynical.

Before they arrived, the oldest of the three sons from the apartment next door came banging on our door. *Kennedy è morto*, he shouted when we opened. Two yards away, at her door, stood his mother, a sturdy woman in an apron—she reminded me of the women in my mother's chorus line—wringing her hands and repeating after him, as in an operatic duet, *Kennedy è morto*. *Venite, venite*, they said. Come in. She waved us into her living room, where on ordinary nights we would sometimes watch television and drink anisette liqueur, but never before in an aura of such drama.

I knew what the words *Kennedy è morto* meant, but the President's death seemed so unlikely that I thought I must have misheard. When they kept repeating it, I assumed Kennedy must have had a heart attack or a stroke. Then they said the word *assassinato,* and then we were in front of the TV, which played the scene over and over. We could see what had happened but couldn't understand the Italian newscasters. So we watched in disbelief, as if this might be happening in Italian but couldn't really be happening in English.

Our friends arrived and came in to watch too. When we returned to our apartment, the translator explained what we had seen. The four of us were horrified but the older Fulbright made jokes about the assassination in his cynical way. At his urging we went out to dinner as planned. I still feel a wisp of guilt that we went out to dinner after such a momentous event, although I'm not sure what we should have done instead.

Because of the older Fulbright's cavalier attitude, the evening left us confused as well as horrified, and it was not until the following day that we began to take in what had happened. We set off for the American Embassy, a big white building with a fence around it on the Via Veneto. We weren't sure why but it seemed the place to go, the closest place to home. There we found dozens of Americans gathered, who had come for the same reason, standing around looking stunned and perplexed.

Later that day we read in the paper that Jack Ruby had shot Lee Harvey Oswald. Again I thought my imperfect Italian must be misleading me, but I read the sentences over and over and there was nothing else they could have meant. At night we saw that killing, too, on our neighbors' TV. This time we had the anisette liqueur along with the news.

After a while we accepted that this dreadful thing had indeed taken place, in every language, and that we would be returning in the spring to a changed country. And before we knew it, it was New Year's Eve and our landlords, the Rosellis, invited us to their annual celebration, along with several genial, stolid middle-aged couples. As far as I can remember, we had never discussed the assassination with our landlords, and it did not come up at the New Year's celebration. In the exuberance of the party, it was as if the tragedy that had stunned us only a few weeks previous in our apartment with the big red bed had never happened. After the lavish dinner, they introduced us to the Roman custom of throwing used household articles out the window at the stroke of midnight. Mostly they threw dishes, also a lamp and some old clothes, and they gave us old pots to throw. We hurled them with abandon and they made a great clatter. Everyone roared with laughter. The Rosellis told us that people strolling around Rome on New Year's Eve were careful to walk in the center of the street so as not to be hit by falling crockery or worse. As we were leaving they wished us well, as usual, with warm exclamations of *"Tante belle cose,"* and we walked home through streets littered with discarded toilets, sinks, chairs, radios, clocks. Our friend from the sanitation department later said that cleaning up after New Year's was a nightmare, an *incubo.*

an ugly house; speaking in tongues

A S IN JAMAICA after the crab races, at some point on every trip I
lie down, stare at the ceiling and ask myself why I've come. I vow
never to leave home again. And yet I break my vow over and over.
Travel always sounds so enticing—the unimaginable newness, the
splendid scenery, the streets, the shops, the people, the whole gorgeous otherness of it all, not to mention the pleasantly distant vision
of one's own waiting life (the suddenly tidy architectural model, too
far away to need managing) and the happy relief of return, the self-
satisfaction of having traveled, not unlike the satisfaction of having
written a book, compared to the strenuousness of actually writing
it. So enticing that I forget what traveling actually entails. Desire
wins out over anxiety; I am not my mother after all. In 1994 I
broke my vow and accepted a teaching job in Honolulu. Who could
refuse Honolulu? The tug of the unknown—what might happen,
how might I change?—the chance of seeing a new ocean, overcame
my natural resistance and I said yes, I'm on my way.

We lived in a large house in a Honolulu suburb. I hadn't lived in a house since my childhood and I liked it more than I expected, only I could never get used to the bedrooms being downstairs. In my childhood house, as in most houses, the bedrooms were upstairs. The house was high-ceilinged, light and spacious, and the sweet, pungent smell of ginger from the plants outside would float into our open windows, along with a flute-like burbling from the nearby brook. Every morning we found tiny translucent oblong specks scattered on the furniture, which we learned were the wings of termites.

To our surprise, the skies were often gray. Hawaii, as everyone knows, is reputed to be perpetually sunny, but here the sky was gray because the suburb lay in a valley enclosed by looming volcanic mountains, scored as if by huge dragons' teeth, and clouds got trapped between the mountains for weeks at a time, waiting for some meteorological shift that would release them. To see the sun we had to drive through a tunnel in the mountains; then we would emerge into Honolulu radiance. The drivers in Hawaii were strikingly polite, always slowing down to make way for merging traffic, then thanking each other for such small courtesies by sticking a hand out the window and wiggling it back and forth, fingers curled, thumb and pinkie up. This endeared them to me. I always fear I'll never be able to merge into the flow of traffic, a fear that may or may not be an emblem of a greater fear about edging my way into the worldly stream of movers and shakers.

That worldly stream did not seem as urgent or as swiftly flowing in Hawaii, which may be why the drivers were so accommodating. Of course this is an outsider's view. For the locals, there were urgencies enough, though the benign climate and the presence of the ocean on all sides couldn't help but smooth the jagged edges of daily life. All the same, the history of Hawaii since Captain Cook neared its shores in 1778 has been one of thorough-going exploitation and oppression. While we were there, many native Hawaiians were engaged in an intense political struggle for sovereignty, that is, independence from the United States, a struggle that rarely found—or finds, since it is ongoing—its way into the mainland media. (A notable recent exception is Elinor Langer's comprehensive essay in the April 28, 2008, issue of *The Nation*, which traces the "discovery" of Hawaii by the West, the subsequent decimation of the native population, the coming of the entrepreneurs and missionaries, and the eventual illegal and forcible assumption of power by the United States Marines, con-cluding with the resulting protests and contemporary sovereignty movement.) These vocal activist groups still bitterly resent the takeover of their country in 1898, when Queen Liliu'okalani was barricaded in her palace and summarily deposed. Overnight, the islands, already in the hands of sugar and pineapple plantation owners, some of them the descendants of missionaries, officially became the property of the United States.

The sovereignty movement was compelling and we followed it keenly, but we were visitors. We had sympathies but no per-manent stake. Our struggles were back home—as are those of all travelers—and so we lived in an artificial bubble of serenity.

At the East-West Center at the University of Hawaii in Manoa, a group of Tibetan monks spent months constructing a large mandala made of colored sand. One Saturday afternoon a crowd gathered to watch them destroy their work, a gorgeous, intricately designed circle of dazzling colors depicting a landscape.

The destruction of the mandala symbolized the acceptance of the transience of all earthly things.

As four monks stood by in their saffron robes, a fifth raised a tool that resembled a giant pizza cutter and sliced into the mandala. He sliced and sliced, till the colors vanished and dispersed into the dull shade of common sand. After many slices had ruined the mandala, the monks, looking quite cheerful as they administered the coup de grace, ran their hands over it until it was nothing but a heap of sand. Then they put handfuls of this plain sand into little Ziploc baggies and offered a bag to each person in the crowd. It was supposed to bring good luck. I didn't want a baggie of tan sand. I wanted the mandala back in all its splendor, even if that meant I couldn't accept the transience of earthly things. But I took one when it was offered, so as not to appear rude or disrespectful or spiritually undeveloped. I knew I could never destroy my own work as blithely as they did.

One day shortly after the destruction of the mandala, amid the scent of ginger and the burbling of the brook and under the gray sky, I got a phone call inviting me to teach in St. Louis. I almost laughed aloud at the prospect but again, good manners saved me from myself and instead I thanked the caller and said I would like to think it over.

I told Harry about the offer, offhandedly, as something obviously out of the question. I had never had fantasies of going to St. Louis. All I knew of it was the song and the Judy Garland movie and the arch. He didn't see it as out of the question. He thought my teaching in St. Louis was not only feasible but might be a very good idea, and moreover I could ask if perhaps there was a job available for him too. This way, he reasoned, we could have an adventure in a new place and earn some money and he could explore contacts in the Midwest for his consulting practice, a prospect that, to his irritation, I took to calling expanding his power base. There were all these fine potential benefits, according to him, while to me it simply meant more travel—I was hardly used to living in Hawaii, beautiful as it was—and this time to a place not especially known for excitement and far from any ocean. The ocean, as I have said, was a necessity, not only so I could sit on the sand staring out at the water, but for the prospect of freedom. The ocean is a path to elsewhere, and thus an emblem of hope.

After some discussion I agreed to ask the people in St. Louis if they might have a job for Harry as well. This would satisfy him, I thought, and seemed safe: it was very unlikely to work out. The university might not even have an urban planning department, and if it did, why would that department hire a new faculty member who, despite his exemplary consulting background, did not have much teaching experience? Besides, it would require inter-departmental hassling that no one would care to undertake. So I made my acceptance dependent on a job for him. Many calls and letters ensued, and then interviews and negotiations that I unwittingly set in motion. Before I knew it, we were both working in St. Louis.

The husband following the wife's job was a switch from the earlier years of our marriage, when women packed up and without a second thought went wherever their husbands' work took them. I had done this when I was young: first to Philadelphia, where Harry attended graduate school and I typed at the American Friends Service Committee, then to Boston where I worked at a magazine, and finally to Rome for the Fulbright year, where I learned how to say, "Does this apartment have central heating?" in Italian, and taught English to high school girls hoping to find secretarial jobs in American corporations.

This time my job was the impetus for our move, yet I went with a sense of disbelief and wonder that it was happening at all. For one thing, the major attraction was gone before I even arrived. I had looked forward to working with Stanley Elkin, talking about soap and books and gossiping about students and colleagues. Maybe I would learn something; maybe I would become a wilder writer, like him. On earlier visits I had grown fond of him. His blunt and unforgiving manner and the outrageous things he said reminded me of my family (my father's side, that is, the side I suspected was related to Ariel Sharon), so I felt at home in his house with all the soap. But he died just before I got there.

Harry and I taught in St. Louis for three successive spring semesters, from January to early May. It's called spring, but most of the stretch is winter. Each year we pondered where to live, hoping for the ideal arrangement. The first year we stayed in a residential hotel in a neighborhood touted as the heart of the action. We had read somewhere that looking out your window from this building you would see "a grand parade" on the street below. But no matter what hour of the day or night we looked, we never saw more than three or four people at a time.

The day we arrived was an unseasonably warm Sunday in January, so after we unloaded our things Harry suggested we take a walk and check out this bustling center. We walked and walked down deserted streets of shabby residential houses until we realized we were going in the wrong direction. The parade must be elsewhere. It was disconcerting that Harry had made that error, as he has a preternaturally accurate sense of direction, so accurate that in any city or country he can find his way back to places he visited five, ten, or twenty years previous. In Madrid not long ago he strode, as if by radar, to a restaurant we had liked sixteen years earlier. It must be an innate sense of orientation in the physical world, a kind of built-in north arrow. That it failed on our first day in St. Louis felt like an omen. By the time we realized our error it was too late to go seeking a parade, so we turned back to settle into our new quarters.

This did fulfill one of my childhood dreams, since we were living in a hotel, or a quasi-hotel. A residential hotel. Our furnished apartment was undistinguished: boxy furniture, blank gray walls, gray institutional carpeting. I tried to spiff up its drabness by hanging pictures and tossing colorful scarves here and there, but nothing could really mitigate that industrial carpeting underfoot. Downstairs, however, the lobby resembled the hotel lobbies I had imagined in my youth. There was a doorman. There were soft armchairs and low tables, potted plants, rugs, chandeliers. There were people at the desk who greeted us as we went in and out, and whom we got to know. I liked being known by the desk clerks. I liked the small services they performed—receiving packages or calling upstairs when we had visitors. The building had a miniature exercise room with a few treadmills and weight machines, and sometimes I would drop in there for twenty minutes or so to use the treadmill and feel virtuous. I liked achieving a sense of virtue without having to put on my coat.

We made friends at school who suggested that the next year we find a sublet belonging to some wandering professor and his family. They were cautious about locations, though. Certain neighborhoods were to be avoided. I was used to my Manhattan neighborhood with its mix of faces, skin colors, and languages, so it took me a while to realize that St. Louis was still very racially segregated. Some areas, our advisors hinted, were not suitable for white people. The longer I stayed in St. Louis the more I realized just how divided a city it was. The downtown had several theatres but people from the university didn't go there much. A local joke claimed that the professors and their families went to Europe more often than they went downtown. At a concert given by the St. Louis Symphony we saw a row of policemen escorting the suburban attendees from the parking lot to the adjacent theatre.

The second year we sublet from a professor who was traveling, and it was in this house—highly recommended—that the misery of displacement got me in a chokehold. Living in the house was a drawn-out version of my nighttime awakening in Orkos, except that it gripped me in the day as well as the night, and was punctuated by intermittent spells of sanity, whenever I was out of the house.

It stood on a quiet street amid other unprepossessing single-family houses and from the outside was not exceptionally ugly, just a little, in the ordinary way. It was the inside that had the aggressive ugliness of certain surrealist art or installations.

We got to know the absent family—father, mother, and little girl, to judge by the extensive doll collection—quite well during our stay. This knowledge took a while to accumulate. But very quickly, in the first fifteen minutes, two salient traits were clear. First, they were collectors. Second, they had a passion for layering.

Every surface was covered several times over. The living room and dining room floors were shielded by powder-blue mats laid on diagonal paths; beneath the powder-blue mats were clear plastic mats. On the windows, upstairs and down, hung powder-blue brocade curtains lined with net curtains, gray with dust. The dust on the Venetian blinds in the tiny brown-wallpapered TV room was so thick it didn't even stir when you blew on it. The dust was layered too, as were the edges of the bookshelves, which were lined with cassettes, paper clips, pads, ballpoint pens, and plastic toothpick containers, creating a barrier to the books.

Aside from stacks of chessboards and cartons of records, the living room held very little—just two black fake-leather couches facing each other as if in feeble hopes of conversation. The walls, papered in gilt, were decorated with Mexican sombreros, one with a bunch of purple plastic grapes affixed to the brim.

The pale blue Formica kitchen counters had rounded edges, which ensured that anything placed near the edge would roll off onto the sticky linoleum floor. The drawers were so stuffed with cooking utensils of all sizes and shapes that you could barely open them. Tupperware crammed the microwave. Beneath the sink huddled a jumble of cleaning equipment in plastic and metal cans, plus sponges, rubber gloves, and several half-empty tissue boxes. Likewise, the refrigerator: when we first opened it, we were so aghast that we had to close it immediately and compose ourselves. It was bursting with jars and plastic containers, none of which appeared to hold anything edible. In the overflowing fruit bins lurked hardened objects resembling the samples of ore sold in New York City's Museum of Natural History, all neatly wrapped in layers of plastic.

Upstairs, the wall-to-wall carpeting, stained and blotchy and of indeterminate color, gray, or gray-green, or gray-blue, felt soft and spongy underfoot, like walking on a tongue. The green, diseased tongue of the house. A vertiginous wallpaper of white cherry blossoms on tarnished gold enclosed the bedroom, interspersed with mirrors, which made us wonder if they watched themselves in bed. In the closets we found an impressive collection of wire and plastic hangers, each batch scrupulously tied with string, heaped in plastic laundry baskets. A supplementary stash of cleaning equipment was stored under the bathroom sink, together with bars of soap (not the miniatures I like to collect), empty pill bottles, and a shoebox of equipment for the removal of earwax.

But all this paled compared to the basement. A shadowy staircase lined with overflowing shelves led down to a dim vault with a bumpy, pocked, blue-gray cement floor. It was lit by a series of bulbs with dangling strings, but the strings didn't work; you had to turn the bulbs slightly in their sockets, and when they lit up, a burst of heat warmed your palm. Here in the bowels of the house, as in a museum cellar, were several world-class collections: plastic bags, from the sleek, shiny kind with the logos of fancy shops to the cheap, crinkly kind that makes a metallic sound when squeezed. Then the lint collection: a sizable bag stuffed with balls of lint from the dryer as well as the damp slime balls that gather in the filter of the washing machine. Years' worth of dust balls were patiently drying out, emitting that special laundry lint smell, simultaneously clean and musty. The oil collection: rows of ancient, dust-covered bottles of Karo syrup, olive oil, sesame oil, chili oil, all with that inimitable sticky blend of dust and oil that clings to the fingers. Finally, in a far corner was piled a collection of vacuum cleaner parts and mops, alongside a lifetime supply of tampons, Kotex, and panty liners in every size and degree of absorbency. No cheap hotel from our salad days had ever instilled in me such profound anomie as this infernal house.

The third year we were more choosy about subletting, and found a congenial house, except that it came with a cat. We had never had a cat and never wished for one, but for the sake of the house, with some trepidation we accepted the cat as well. We quickly grew fond of him—an eighteen-pound marmalade cat who slept with us and greeted us every evening by rolling on the rug at the door, and sat on the table while we ate, a habit we didn't like but couldn't manage to extirpate. So that house did provide an adventure of a sort, becoming intimate with a cat. Later on I wrote an essay about my relationship with the cat, so I felt I had gotten something useful out of living there. As my friend who studied the *Tao te Ching* with me remarks whenever one of us is going through a trying time: remember, one day this will become literature. (Though not quite the kind of literature Stendhal or Byron made of their travels.) The trials are not necessarily redeemed, but at least they are put to use, and attain a life beyond and better than their origins.

Living in other people's houses as we did in St. Louis and Hawaii, getting to know their domestic habits—that some people save lint, for instance, or keep a refrigerator beside the bed, or buy designer toys for cats, or label every shelf with Dymotape strips listing the contents—made me realize that anyone who stayed in our house must be gathering similar information. For often while traveling, we had sublet our New York City apartment or invited friends to use it.

Did they go through the bathroom cabinets and assemble a medical profile? What did they make of Harry's collection of Wash 'n Dries, or mine of miniature shampoos? Of the 1960s black-and-white TV in the bedroom? Did they evaluate the food in the freezer? There was that old turkey bone from a Thanksgiving dinner that I had been planning to use for a soup some day: by now it was surely a fossil. Not to mention files, old checkbooks, letters, mementos, all awaiting the indiscreet eye. How easy it would be to cobble together a story of our lives, an unflattering and distorted story. It does makes you wonder about biographers, who piece together life stories from such artifacts, stories that might well be unrecognizable to their subjects, stories that omit all the things that are undocumented and exist only in the privacy of the mind, shaping our conceptions of ourselves.

Cee

No one ransacking the detritus of my life would guess at my fantasies of being Italian, or at least of having a handful of Italian genes. Shortly before he died in his late nineties, Uncle Bert of the wanderlust, who uncannily resembled Ariel Sharon, undertook to compile a family tree. What with migrations and pogroms and abandoned or non-existent records, this is no easy task for Jewish immigrants from Eastern Europe, and Bert's tree—wider than it was high—got only as far back as his parents, my grandparents. When he presented copies of the tree to everyone in our large family, I saw that my grandmother's original family name was

Nuzzi, a Northern Italian name. If she really was Italian, as I like to think, how and when did she find her way to the small town outside of Kiev where she married my grandfather—possibly an arranged marriage? Is it because of her that I feel at home in Italy and that the language came easily to my tongue?

I had acquired a reading knowledge of Italian in graduate school, but I began to speak it only during the Fulbright year, with the help of the translator who came over the night of Kennedy's assassination. Over the years my spoken Italian has ranged from adequate on good days to primitive on bad, depending on when I last visited there, or whether I've kept up with reading or done any translations. After a few days in Italy, invariably the language comes tumbling back; phrases catapult into my head; I even start thinking in Italian.

But whatever the level of my speech, without fail I take on a different personality, or persona, in Italian than I have in English. I think this must be true of anyone who speaks more than one language, and has little to do with proficiency or the lack of it. Just as we may have a repertoire of selves for home or abroad, for work or play or love, the self is inflected by each language we speak. If it doesn't alter intrinsically, at the very least it changes its costume. In Italian my costume is brighter, lighter, more flamboyant and exuberant. I become outgoing, bold—a kind of merry tipsiness. Likewise, on the rare occasions when I speak French, a chilly reserve infuses me, a mixture of shyness and hauteur, a retreat to more somber colors and tailored lines. I much prefer my Italian self and often wish I could carry it over into English, but I think it derives from the language itself. The self changes shape according to the movements of the tongue and the receptors of the ear, just as the body grows languid or stiffens when we travel to a warm or cold climate.

I've seen the cities and the terraced countryside, I've read some history and fiction, and I speak the language after a fashion. I've been in friends' houses and know enough now to sense who they are. But do I really know anything at all about Italy? When I tell Italian friends that I'd like to find an apartment and settle in Rome, they say I don't know what I'm talking about. Have I any idea of the political corruption, the grip of the Mafia, the influence of the Catholic Church, how difficult it is to get a repairman or have a telephone installed? And this is a country I lived in for a year and visited half a dozen times since that first trip when we took showers at the Albergo Diurno.

The dilemma of travel is one of epistemology. What does it mean to know a country other than one's own? What do tourists know, who come home with photographs and scattershot anecdotes? Anything at all? Sinclair Lewis, writing in *Dodsworth,* would say no:

> Since the days of Alexander the Great there has been a fashionable belief that travel is agreeable and highly educative. Actually, it is one of the most arduous yet boring of all pastimes and, except in the case of a few experts who go globe-trotting for special purposes, it merely provides the victim with more topics about which to show ignorance.

What can I claim to know after my week in Mexico? Any more than what a visitor to the United States would know after reading *101 American Customs*, which portrays our country as a land of Tupperware parties, demolition derbies, eating contests, square dancing, an apple for the teacher, and the Sadie Hawkins dance? I saw magnificent ruins and dutifully read about their origins. I ate delicious food. I bought dresses in the open-air market in Oaxaca. I spoke tourist Spanish with waiters, taxi drivers, and the staff of a splendid hotel converted from an old convent, a hotel that a few years later I rediscovered in Italo Calvino's story, "Under the Jaguar Sun," about a couple on a trip to Mexico, just like us.

As I read it, the setting began to sound very familiar, especially the description of the hotel dining room, in an outdoor courtyard with palm trees and adobe walls. I've been there, I thought with a happy jolt. That was our very hotel. I've sat in that courtyard, on those very wicker chairs. I've felt the breeze stirred by those palm fronds. I've eaten the food Calvino describes so zestfully, food that for his narrator evokes ancient rites of cannibalism as well as a heated eroticism.

The story is so vivid that I might almost have learned as much about Mexico by reading it as I did in my week as a tourist. True, I wouldn't have the colorful dresses. I wouldn't have tasted the spices he writes about—the sensual mystery and history of food are his subject—or climbed the steps of the ruins in the punishing sun. I wouldn't have had so much pure sensory pleasure, and I wouldn't feel a longing to return someday. For I would like to go back to Mexico. (I would even like to go back to Greece, notwithstanding Orkos.) Or rather, I would like not to "go" to Mexico but to *be* there, transported without any physical movement or tedious arrangements, and once I find myself magically there, to have an apartment and a grocery store, friends and a job—that is, a life. To be anything but a tourist, which is a false position that cannot be sustained very long without fragmenting the self. In my case that takes about three days.

On the trip to South Africa where I looked for the border of two oceans, I met a young American woman who was well-traveled; she'd spent months in rented apartments in various European cities. As we talked about this matter of knowing a place, she said she always described her visits very carefully. She would say she'd "stayed" in Lisbon or Nice or Antwerp rather than "lived" there. Her brief sojourns, always temporary and uncommitted—never demanding that she shoulder the burdens or shames of citizenship—didn't seem to her to have earned the word "lived."

Calvino's Kublai Khan finds himself in another kind of epistemological trap: he's amassed so much territory that he can no longer comprehend it:

> In the lives of the emperors, there is a moment which follows pride in the boundless extension of the territories we have conquered, and the melancholy and relief of knowing we shall soon give up any thought of knowing and understanding them.

That happens to me when I see too much in too brief a time. It happened on that recent trip to Sicily, the trip I almost didn't make because I left my passport in a book on the living-room coffee table. Harry and I visited five cities in less than two weeks, a foolish pace I'd vowed never to agree to again, but as usual I broke my vow. I remember it was the city of Noto that had the magnificent baroque architecture, and Agrigento where we wandered for a day among the classical Greek ruins. But as for our incomparable dinners in a restaurant jutting out over the sea, or the romantic twilight stroll along a cypress-lined pier—I can't say for sure where they took place. I remember the stark trapezoidal shape of a sixteenth-century piazza, its massive old buildings hung with colorful banners, its cafés crowded with chattering people, the buzz of Vespas and the clink of coffee cups, but I have to think hard to recall exactly where it was. This is not knowledge, just bits of disassembled data. It is not even true recollection of experience, but rather a kaleidoscopic blur, the opposite of the stillness from which memory is nourished and wisdom—as the *Tao te Ching* tells us—is born. I should have taken notes, I suppose, or better still, turned the trip into a story.

Habitual travelers may confront the same dilemma. Having conquered, or set foot in, so many places, the result might be not an orderly atlas of acquired knowledge, but a spreading chaos. "Only in Marco Polo's accounts was Kublai Khan able to discern . . . the tracery of a pattern so subtle it could escape the termites' gnawing." Only through stories—that is, through the transforming work of the imagination—can we have any glimpse of the world's coherence. And so to find out about Marco Polo himself, I'd sooner read Calvino's novel than the explorer's own journals.

Since my way of knowing anything is more through language than seeing, I try to learn some of the language before I go anywhere. To be unable to ask a simple question or read the street signs would be the equivalent, for me, of visual types having to travel with gauze over their eyes. Not that they would be completely blinded, but they would see the world through a kind of sieve; the finer particles would slip away, leaving only the grosser.

There was in fact a famous blind traveler, James Holman, an Englishman born in 1777 who may have covered more miles—250,000, according to his biographer, Jason Roberts—than any other traveler in history. Certainly more than Marco Polo, with his alleged 14,000. For some of those miles Holman traveled with a companion who was deaf.

Once a Royal Navy lieutenant, James Holman lost his vision at the age of twenty-five, but refused to accept the constraints of blindness. After attending medical school, he set out to circumnavigate the globe—by ship, on horseback, and on foot with the aid of a walking stick—and nearly accomplished his goal. He did make it to every continent, enjoying many adventures with women he met along the way.

His explicit purpose was that of all serious travelers: "to explore distant regions, to trace the varieties exhibited by mankind." His originality, apart from his extraordinary courage, was in grasping that this might be accomplished by methods other than seeing. Using a device called a Noctograph, which made his writing legible, he kept copious journals and published three books recounting his trips. For a while these were widely read, but by the fourth volume his public had evidently had enough. Like many writers who fall out of favor, though, he persevered, and spent his final years working on *Holman's Narratives of His Travels*. He died at seventy, in 1857, and his unpublished work was lost.

Holman sounds like the perfect candidate for an Oliver Sacks essay, but unfortunately no one like Sacks was around at the time to engage so intimately and eloquently with the texture of his daily experience. Public attitudes and discourse about physical deficits were light years away from today's sophistication—and politeness—nor were there advocacy groups for the disabled.

The current therapeutic culture may be tainted by naïveté and psychobabble, but at least it fosters a civilized approach to people overcoming disabilities—witness the Special Olympics, or the New York City Marathon where bystanders whoop and cheer for "runners" in wheelchairs. Back in Holman's day the disabled could be dismissed with impunity. One reader found his writings "incongruous and approaching the absurd. . . . His memoranda . . . cannot have authenticity enough to warrant their obtrusion on the public." I haven't read the journals, but I imagine they could stand up to similar testimonies from the sighted, and might be instructive in unexpected ways.

Luckily I do not travel blind—so far—but like Holman I get my information from what people say and how they sound. So I study the grammar books and phrase books before I pack, longing all the while that I could be like the W. G. Sebald character who "had the special gift of acquiring a foreign language, without apparent effort and without any teaching aids, within a year or two, solely by making certain adjustments . . . to his inner self." Sometimes I have an inkling of what those adjustments must be; I even feel I'm on the verge of making them, but then I'm defeated by the case endings of an inflected adjective, or the irregularities of a pesky verb.

Even without such mysterious gifts, from repeating the words aloud and feeling them take shape in my mouth, I grasp something of what the people and the place are like, the same way that a scholar decoding a few glyphs can deduce, or intuit, the nature of the entire document, and maybe even the lost civilization. The syllables the speakers are accustomed to shaping, how they must move their mouths and tongues, the sorts of lingual dexterity they possess: all these add up to a kind of intimacy. And after the sounds come the grammar and syntax—how the phrases are built and fit together like Lego segments, the hierarchical priorities of the parts of speech. Together these reveal the architecture of the collective sensibility.

Language maps the topography of the mind. It creates the ambience in which we think; it determines what thoughts are possible and impossible, which cognitive byways are preferred and which closed off, what detours must be made. Yoko Tawada notes this with her typical acidic whimsy: "Often it sickened me to hear people speak their native tongues fluently. It was as if they were unable to think and feel anything but what their language so readily served up to them." She is no less harsh on herself and her own language, Japanese. While she's visiting Germany,

> most of the words that came out of my mouth had nothing to do with how I felt. But at the same time I realized that my native tongue didn't have words for how I felt either. It's just that this never occurred to me until I'd begun to live in a foreign language.

A student at a writers' conference once asked me and a famous poet how much of what one feels can be expressed in words. Ninety percent, I said blithely. Ten percent, said the poet. Whether we are overly optimistic or pessimistic, these inadequate words are what we have. They are the stuff our questions about the world are made of.

Once you know the rudiments of a new language, a miniature window opens and you can glimpse the square it frames. It's like getting past the customs inspectors and out into the street. In St. Petersburg, like everyone else I was excited by the white nights, by the Hermitage, by the great square where the revolution began. But I was even more excited to be able to decipher a plaque on a building not far from our hostel. It took me about fifteen minutes to read the plaque, which finally yielded up the fact that the nineteenth-century composer Alexander Glazunov had lived in that building. I had heard Glazunov's music. Now I looked at his former residence, the street he walked down every day. I saw what he had seen. I fit a few pieces of an infinite puzzle together. I possessed a tiny piece of genuine knowledge.

Essential as I find it, a smattering of an unfamiliar language can also lead you astray. In Greece, if you ask a question, an affirmative answer is *"ne,"* pronounced "neh." Or as the guidebook puts it in boldface capital letters, NO MEANS YES. To confuse matters further, *"ne"* is sometimes spoken in a way that makes it seem like "no," that is, with a slight tilt of the head. All the time I was in Athens I tried to bear in mind that no means yes. I hailed a taxi and in hesitant Greek asked the driver if he knew the route to my hotel, which was on an obscure street. *"Ne, ne,"* he said. I was encouraged and got in. But he kept saying *"ne"* until it dawned on me that he was saying "no." He could see that I was American and was trying to accommodate me in English. So sometimes *"ne"* means "no."

a hand in the water

A T SOME POINT I said no to visiting Uncle Bert. My visits had dropped off, partly because I'd gotten used to the vacancy my father's death left in the world and was not quite so much in need of hearing his voice or seeing the planes and angles of his long, sallow face. Indeed my father, who was such a vivid presence for me in his lifetime, after his death began fading like a Polaroid photo going in the wrong direction, from color and definition back to milky blur. I once thought I knew him through and through, each atom; I had studied him with critical scrutiny, as daughters do. Now I'm not sure I knew anything at all except the surface. Now, unless I make a conscious effort to locate the particles of him that lodged in me, he's like someone I used to see around all the time but never knew very well. Certain people need to be physically present in order to be fully apprehended. My mother remains as vivid as when I last saw her alive. I know her better now than I did then.

But there was another reason I said no. During the height of my visiting, Bert said he would like to take my family out to dinner. We should choose the place, the most expensive restaurant we could find. I didn't know any very expensive restaurants at the time, so on a friend's recommendation I suggested a new French restaurant on the East Side. It was an unfortunate choice, or night, because the place was nearly empty, which seemed a reflection on my savoir faire, and to make matters worse they didn't have the dish Bert ordered. Salmon. Poached. He berated the waiter loudly, making an awful scene with his demands for the salmon, and I was mortified. My daughters, in early adolescence—this was shortly after they realized that the younger one was taller than the older—looked on in astonishment.

When we left I swore that I would never again appear in a public place with Bert. I was newly grateful that my mother had not married him. My father had been capable of public rudeness too, but only with significant provocation. The absence of his chosen dish on the menu would not have been sufficient to trip the wires, so to speak. It would have taken something more significant, a friend's betrayal, perhaps, or a remark showing political ingenuousness. Then he would stomp around shouting his bitter views: that religion was the opiate of the people, that altruism was the mask of self-interest, and that the Marshall Plan was less generosity than a way of insuring eventual markets for American goods. "Markets, markets, it's all markets," he would sputter, waving his arms in the air and making small objects in the vicinity tremble.

Then again, my father would never have found himself in such an expensive restaurant: he hated that kind of pretension.

He wasn't willing to pay for "atmosphere," he always said, just for food. So my visits to Bert tapered off in the wake of that disastrous evening, which is no doubt why I never cruised down the Amazon.

In December of 2006 three new biographies of Ariel Sharon appeared. I read the reviews. Sharon's family came from Soviet Georgia; mine came from a town near Kiev. His original family name was Scheinerman, which was not my family's original name. "The Hebraicized name," one reviewer writes, "was given to him by David Ben-Gurion, like a Shakespearean king anointing one of his knights." Thus ended our hypothetical kinship.

After our Roman landlords' hospitality, after the piano, the picnic, and throwing the pots out the window on New Year's Eve, the countless repetitions of "*Tante belle cose*"—so many beautiful things—it was something of a bitter surprise when Signor Vito, one evening towards the end of our stay, grew nostalgic for the military police of the Fascist era, the *bersaglieri* in their crisp, spotless white uniforms. How splendid they looked in the old days, he said in his hoarse voice, his broad face beaming, as they marched in step down the avenue. By this time we understood almost everything he said. We listened, dazed, uncertain how to respond, or whether to respond at all. I tried to frame some suitable remarks, but wavered— my Italian was not up to the task of outlining the evils of Fascism, or linking the splendor of the pageantry to the crimes of the regime. In the end we sat stiffly, waiting for him to wind down.

Had we unwittingly taken up with neo-Fascists or was this innocent nostalgia? No nostalgia is really innocent, at least it shouldn't be. It is the apparent innocence of certain modes of nostalgia that makes them suspect. How innocent or ignorant could Signor Vito be? He was delivering his speech about half a mile from the great Roman synagogue, centerpiece of the Ghetto, from which, on the morning of October 16, 1943, a few days after the Armistice, over a thousand Jews were carried off—not precisely by the white-uniformed *bersaglieri* Signor Vito missed but by their provisional colleagues, the occupying Nazi soldiers. The story is told in a famous essay, "October 16, 1943," by the literary critic, Giacomo Debenedetti. It was first published in December 1944, in the journal *Mercurio,* and didn't come out in book form until 2001, with an introduction by Natalia Ginzburg.

A week before October 16, the German commanding officer, one Major Kappler, had summoned the leaders of the Jewish community to demand a ransom. "The Roman Jews, he said, were doubly guilty: as Italians, and thus traitors, and as Jews, and thus centuries-old enemies of Germany," writes Ginzburg. He stipulated fifty kilos of gold, to be raised and presented within a day and a half. Even though the residents of the Ghetto were mostly poor working families or owners of small businesses, somehow this sum was raised. And once it was handed over, the Jews of the Ghetto were relieved. Then, on the evening of Friday, October 15, a Jewish cleaning woman who lived and worked across the river in Trastevere (where we lived in the apartment with the big red bed, owned by Signor Vito), came running to the Ghetto with a desperate message. Her employer had heard from her husband, a police officer, that the Germans had compiled a list of names of Jewish families to be deported.

"Believe me," the cleaning woman shouted. "Run, I'm telling you. I swear it's the truth. I swear on my children's heads." She was dressed in black, disheveled, slovenly, soaked from the rain.

> She could barely get the words out, she was so choked with agitation, practically foaming at the mouth. . . . No one would believe her; they laughed at her. . . . Everyone knew she was a prattler, a hothead, a fanatic: look how she waved her arms around as she spoke, with those wild staring eyes under that head of hair like a horse's mane. Her whole family was slightly touched—it was common knowledge.

So they carried on with their lives as usual.

That night the silence was ripped by the crackle of gunshots in the street, soldiers' marching feet and furious cries, "voices enraged, sarcastic, incomprehensible." Everyone woke up and peeked fearfully from behind the window curtains. After a while, the streets grew quiet, and once more people convinced themselves that the worst was over. In the morning the soldiers were back, banging on doors and bursting into apartments with their lists. Families were given twenty minutes to gather their essential belongings and assemble in the street, where they were shoved onto trucks. (Earlier, the entire library of the Rabbinical College of Rome, housed in the synagogue and containing countless manuscripts documenting the history of the Jews in Rome, whom Debenedetti calls the "most direct descendents of ancient Judaism," had also been carried off in trucks.)

The young German soldiers who drove the trucks were thrilled to have such vehicles at their disposal, even if they were loaded with rounded-up Jews, and took the opportunity to have a tour of the city. So that the wretches inside had to endure the most whimsical roaming about. . . . Naturally, the favorite destination of these tourists was St. Peter's Square, where several of the trucks remained for some time.

While the Germans marveled at the sight, the passengers shouted pleas to the Pope to come to their aid. "Then the trucks left, and even this last hope evaporated." Finally the Jews were crowded into the Military College, where they remained overnight. And then the trains.

Today, Jews in Rome's Ghetto are again being forced out, not brutally by Nazi soldiers but incrementally by rising property values. A Roman real-estate agent quoted in *The New York Times* said in January 2007, that Ghetto apartments were selling for $1,000 a square foot. "It's only for tourists, for people on magazine covers."

The Ghetto was established in 1555 by papal bull, to contain the city's Jews; its gates were locked at night. That restriction ended in 1870 with Italy's unification, but most of the Jews remained where their lives and livelihoods had taken root. After the Second World War, the Ghetto, with its central location, its imposing synagogue, its winding narrow streets and peeling ocher buildings, became a tourist attraction. With the economic boom of the '60s and then the advent of the European Union, it transmuted into a coveted piece of real estate. Nowadays, many longtime residents are accepting the millions of euros offered for their apartments. "It could be that there is an offer you can't say no to," as one puts it. Still, those who can't afford to resist the offers return daily to run their businesses and sit in the cafes, so that the old life continues in a hybrid form. What began as a place of confinement has evolved into the chic, and the Ghetto Jews, the oldest such community in Europe, have become commuters to their former prison.

"All of us, when we walk through that neighborhood today," writes Ginzburg, "recall that October 16, when hatred and calamity descended on the streets, on people going about their business unawares, ignorant."

I didn't know about the October 16 massacre when Signor Vito lamented the disappearance of the Fascist *bersaglieri*. It wasn't until later that I explored the synagogue and learned about the deportees. Not until forty years after that was Debenedetti's book published and sent to me by an Italian friend. I didn't say anything to Signor Vito at the time, and I don't know what I would have said had I known. It was spring when he talked about the *bersaglieri*; the bright sunshine and balmy air reminded him of the outdoor spectacle he missed. Even in the warm weather, we shivered. But we were getting ready to go home. We were young and ignorant. We listened until he was done, and then changed the subject and left soon after. *Tante belle cose.*

C℘

The day before I was to leave Jamaica I lay on my chair in the shade of the hut inhaling the strong aroma of coconut. That smell is fine when it comes from the fruit but slightly sickening on human skin.

The tourists were conscientiously applying tanning lotions to their bodies, even to their eyelids and the soles of their feet, the backs of the knees and the insides of the elbows, as if offering themselves extreme unction. Forgive us for being who we are, white, well-off, and for provoking and accepting the barely-veiled hostility of our hosts. For gorging ourselves on the fruits that women carry on their heads in the heat of the day, the meat from goats herded by five-year-old goatherds.

I got up and swam in the warm aqua water. As I walked out of the sea, the water chest-high, something happened that I have not been able to explain to myself to this day. I tripped over something. A rock, a crab, I thought. But it felt softer than that. I was surprised, because the bottom was always quite smooth except for a few pebbles. I looked down. The water was so clear I could see to the ocean floor. Shimmering there was a blob about the size of a human hand. I put my head in the water, then dove down to have a closer look. It seemed to be a human hand. White, not large. A woman's hand. My mouth opened and my throat filled with water. I stood up, coughed and sputtered until I could breathe again. Unless I was hallucinating, something terrible had happened here. I must pick up the hand and bring it to the guard. I put my head underwater again. The thing seemed to have moved slightly; maybe it was a weird sort of fish. A skate—they're white and flat. But no, the fingers—what looked like fingers—jiggled with the movement of the water, as if they were practicing scales on the recorder. I couldn't make myself reach for it.

I ran back to shore and told the first person I saw, an elderly man who'd been in the taxi from the airport. He went to tell the guard, and soon a crowd gathered, questioning me. Each time I repeated what I had seen, or imagined, I sounded more flustered and unreliable, like a witness in a TV crime show being badgered on the stand, who crumples in defeat.

"Not possible," the guard said. "Such things do not happen here. No accidents and no drowning. Never. It was a crab you saw. We have very large crabs with tentacles like fingers. Harmless, though," he assured the tourists.

Still, people insisted he send someone into the water to look. A young man in blue trunks appeared, one of the waiters who served at breakfast. He followed me into the water. "Where?" he asked grimly, and I tried to guide him to the place. But it's hard to find an exact spot in an ocean, almost as hard as defining an ocean's borders, and I hadn't thought to look for markers. We swam around underwater for a while, finding nothing, no hand, only a few rocks and a small dead crab. Eventually the swimmers went back into the water. I lay on my beach chair for a while, then slunk off to my room.

Drowsing, I had another of those moments that come to travelers at the start of a trip, and sometimes in the middle or the end. Who am I and what am I doing here? Time passed. Outside my window the sky darkened. It was turning into one of the ten percent afternoons. Rain pattered down onto the terrace. It was true that the drops fell very slowly. I could breathe in between the drops. The wide, slow spaces between the drops held something, some dread or menace so evanescent it could barely show itself anywhere other than the space between raindrops. Something ancient, stale and weary, with a metallic smell, yet sharp, like the razor blades worn on chains around the necks of the young men who paraded up and down the beach with attaché cases, trying to persuade the tourists to buy shell jewelry.

What had I seen and what could it mean? Maybe it was the boys surrounding me on the road, or the silent woman in the windowless bar who sold us sodas, or the somber groups of ragged people watching us ride by on horseback, or just the dizzying smell of cocoa butter seeping into the pale skins that had discombobulated me. But I could have sworn it was a hand.

That was one of the few times water betrayed me. I had always considered water benign. The image of water runs through the *Tao te Ching* as an "emblem of the unassertive." Indeed, "the supreme good is like water, / which nourishes all things without trying to. / It is content with the low places that people disdain."

That view would not be shared by the victims of New Orleans' Hurricane Katrina in 2005, or of the 2004 tsunami in Southeast Asia, or of the periodic flooding of the Mississippi and other great rivers. Water can be both benign and deadly, and not always in relation to its quantity. The will that drives it is indifferent. In another verse, the *Tao te Ching* says, "Nothing in the world / is as soft and yielding as water. / Yet for dissolving the hard and inflexible, nothing can surpass it."

That night, my last on the island, I went down to the beach. Not a soul was around. Except for the lapping water, there was no movement. I'd always found the ocean the best the natural world has to offer, far exceeding the mountains or claustrophobic woodsy settings so beloved by the Romantic poets. I thought I was a connoisseur of beaches, from the lush tropical kind before me, its sea now dark but aquamarine by day, to the sterner Cape Cod kind with their immense sloping dunes. But if I couldn't even tell for sure what I had seen in the water, if I was a creature propelled by anxiety and imagination, then I couldn't be sure what I really knew or felt. Was my love of beaches genuine, truly mine, or simply something I'd been taught? Would I have found them beautiful had I lived two hundred years ago, before beaches were definitively promoted to the realm of the "picturesque?" Are our responses to what we see when we travel (or even when we stay at home) genuine, born of our native sensibilities, or are we so primed by received cultural wisdom (not to mention guidebooks) that we never quite *see* without an intervening scrim of learned expectations?

In any event, the historical blindness to the beauty of the sea couldn't have been universal. South Sea Islanders have always been intimate with the sea. Mythic stories of Captain Cook and his fleet nearing the shores of Hawaii in 1778 tell of young girls swimming out to welcome the ships, never dreaming that with those ships came the seeds of their culture's destruction. This romanticized image sounds like an imperial—or Hollywood—invention, used to advantage in the movie made from James Michener's *Hawaii,* where the lithe swimmers glide glamorously through the surging waves. But the islanders probably did swim confidently in a medium they knew and loved. At the same time, in Brighton, seaside vacationers—leading lives the British women adventurers fled from—were venturing into the sea fully dressed, enclosed in bathing machines, wooden rectangular contraptions on wheels, drawn by horses, in order to cool off as primly as possible.

The sand was cool, the sea dark. The thatched huts, unoccupied, looked like short thick trees growing out of the sand. I searched among the stars for the ones I knew. There must be the same stars here, Orion, the Pleiades, Casseopeia. Something touched my elbow. I swung around: it was the guard with his club. A night guard—I'd never seen the same one twice.

"Good evening, Madam. Enjoying the beach by night? Do you like our island so far? Where are you from? How long do you plan to stay? We pride ourselves on our friendliness and on our sunshine. The sun shines ninety percent. . . ."

Soon he strolled away, and I went back to studying the sky. Maybe I could find the Big Dipper. All the other stars seemed re-arranged, but the Big Dipper is easy to find anywhere. And I did find it, its handle hanging downward, about to touch the rim of the sea. The Big Dipper was slipping into the vat of the sea. Soon the ladle would be immersed for the night, until it was ready to fetch up and serve to me and the other tourists the tropical fruits, the morning sun. The hand holding the Big Dipper was the hand that fed us all.

harmony

Very soon after the September 11 attacks on the World Trade Center, I enrolled in an evening course in Harmony. I'd started picking out tunes on the piano when I was four or five years old, and at six I began taking lessons. Even though I took piano lessons for thirteen years and became a fairly decent amateur pianist, and even though I went diligently through all the scales, chords, and arpeggios, I never achieved a coherent understanding of theory and harmony. For years I mused on and off about remedying this lack and even tried on my own with books, but had little success.

The attack itself was so arresting and unanticipated that even Taoist equanimity, had I ever attained it, would not have prepared me. The downtown site was all everyone thought about and talked about that entire autumn. A half mile north, you could see thin curls of smoke still rising, slow and reluctant. When I closed my eyes, the iconic images of the debris lined the insides of my lids. The newspapers were filled with stories of the dead, new and unforgettable gory details coming to light daily, alongside the dense, specious language of political and military maneuvering. One night, I happened to be leafing through a brochure of concerts and courses offered by a local music school and my eye caught a description of the Harmony course. The next minute I was filling out a form in the back of the brochure. I suppose I wanted to focus my attention, if only for two hours a week, on a subject as far as possible from downtown Manhattan. That must have been why I chose that moment, of all the moments since I stopped taking piano lessons, to become a student of Harmony.

The class was held in a building near Lincoln Center that in the daytime served as a public elementary school for children gifted in music. Our room was a first-grade classroom. The walls were lined with the letters of the alphabet in capitals and lowercase, as well as with pictures of animals, their names printed below in that clear typeface used for small children. There were children's drawings hanging on the walls too. In the midst of the mourning outside those walls, the downtown air thick with the smell of smoke bearing the traces of charred flesh, it was soothing to gaze at crayoned pictures of A-frame houses with curling smoke—innocent smoke—wafting from squat chimneys, of daisies and horses and tricycles, trucks and dogs and oceans made of parallel wavy lines.

We didn't sit in the tiny first-grade chairs—they were stacked up against a wall while we used metal folding chairs—yet there was a sense of miniaturization about the class. Everything, including the room itself, was small and enclosed and manageable. At the front, to one side, was an old upright piano. Facing us was an old-fashioned blackboard. Three horizontal rows of chairs were set up, six chairs in each row, but they were not filled. The class had about eight or ten students, but some nights only five or six attended. I never missed a class. It was the happiest time of my week; I looked forward to it.

The teacher was a very animated, slight, good-looking mustached man named Victor, around forty or so. On the first night Victor instructed us to go out and buy a small music notebook, which I duly did, and I took it to class each week, along with pencils with good erasers, feeling that I was back in elementary school, though I enjoyed the Harmony class more than I had ever enjoyed elementary or any other school.

Victor was an ideal teacher. He always arrived promptly. He shimmered with energy and taught with enthusiasm. He moved swiftly and wrote swiftly on the blackboard, his rendering of the notes possessing a dashing grace quite different from my clumsy, childish efforts. He began the course with the most fundamental aspects of theory, the major and minor scales, the chords, the intervals, all of which were familiar to me, but I didn't mind the repetition. I had learned it piecemeal, not in any orderly fashion. Now I loved the order, the diagrams, the mathematical underpinnings, the way everything fit into a stable and superbly logical whole. Victor progressed weekly from the simple to the more complex, making everything clear and manageable. He taught us about the circle of fifths—the major and minor scales arranged in a perfect circle, a rational, balanced miniature universe—and he made it so clear that I thought I could never forget it. But I have forgotten it, mostly.

Along with the technical material, Victor regaled the class with savory anecdotes about music, musicians, and amusing moments and milestones in the history and development of harmony, and I took copious notes in my little notebook. As he spoke, in his witty and animated way, about the intricacies and subtleties and private jokes of harmony, it seemed there was nothing else of importance in the world except this subject, Harmony, which was of surpassing, crucial importance. For those two hours, my attention was heartfelt and thorough. Everything outside was forgotten; it was as if the attacks had never happened. Only harmony existed.

In school I had never been one of those students who crowd around the teacher after class, yet here I often stayed a few extra minutes to ask Victor questions. These were not merely pretexts to prolong the respite, however. I had serious and pressing questions about harmony and felt I could not go home unless my curiosity was satisfied. Today I remember none of these questions or their answers.

Each week he gave us homework. We had to devise simple harmonies—eight or so bars of music—for four voices, bass, tenor, alto, and soprano, which meant making up four little tunes that fit together according to the principles of harmony. I enjoyed doing my homework—not least the very idea of homework—and would do it as soon as I got home after class, so I wouldn't forget the points in the lesson that needed to be incorporated in the homework. Each week Victor would put one person's homework assignment on the blackboard and we would analyze it to see how well it conformed to the principles of harmony. The night he asked for my assignment I was quite excited. I tore it out of my notebook and handed it to him with a flourish, which made him laugh. He dissected my homework, and though it contained a few small infelicities, overall it was fairly successful, and I was as proud as if I were in first grade and had read aloud, to near-perfection, a passage from a Dick and Jane primer. As the term drew to a close, he suggested that we might want to take the next course in the series on Harmony, in which the homework would no doubt be more complicated. I considered taking this course but never did.

I no longer remember any of the other students, yet I think of them, vague warm bodies in the seats around me, as my companions during that awful time when, outside of Tuesday night's Harmony class, the city was grieving and awash in confusion. I still have my little notebook with all my homework assignments and class notes—the one assignment I ripped out to hand to Victor sticking out with its jagged edge. I look at it sometimes, without opening it, and am reminded of that oasis of harmony, Tuesday nights at 6:15, moving from the luminous blue-skied shocked autumn into the cold winter of resignation, through the various kinds of intervals, through consonance and dissonance and inversions, and always the perfect foundation of the circle of fifths, while outside the little room came anthrax and Afghanistan and the daily funerals and the recovery of body parts.

When the course was over I thought maybe it was time to write something again. If I stop writing even for a couple of weeks I worry that I'm not really a writer anymore. I would probably have to write something about what had just happened in New York, because it was a boulder in my mind and nothing else could get past it. But I also remembered those old pages in my desk drawer about the doomed twins from the family on whom, in my loneliness and frustration in southern California, I had heaped tragedy, a tragedy that hadn't added up to anything useful in a literary sense.

I took out those old pages, and in this new context of the terrorist attacks, they made sense. I saw a way they could begin to cohere. As before, one twin would die early on, and the remaining twin's grief would be evoked later as a memory. But the story of her life would have to be redesigned, for along with the private tragedy would be added the greater, public tragedy, the two permeating each other. The narrative would no longer be an assemblage of pointless mayhem, but could take a useful place in the larger world, as an attempt to make a pattern out of what had happened. It would have the context and the purpose it had lacked before. Instead of creeping around the boulder in my mind I would drill my way through it.

So at last I was able to finish my story about the twins. Along the way, I jettisoned the hotel setting. By that time I had stayed in many hotels and was no longer awed by their glamour. But more important, in this new context, hotels no longer mattered. They were like the crumpled up newspaper that you use to set a good log fire and that disappears in the blaze of its own making. Far more significant than hotels were communal grief and shock and their aftermath, the need to undergo and assimilate them. Those would be the core of the story I began at eleven years old in the seventh grade on Friday afternoons at 2:15 in Creative Arts, decades before anyone ever dreamed that the World Trade Center would be built, still less that it would be destroyed one sunny autumn morning.

So I was a writer after all. I was completing what I'd started long ago and would send it out to be read, not by some ghostly double but by strangers. While I was writing I lost all taste for adventure—for venturing out into the world, that is. I had this task to do, and whatever was not that task was time stolen from it. When you are engaged on this journey, real travel is an interruption. You have to cut short your fantasy trip to pack real clothing in real suitcases and set off for someplace unrelated to your primary journey. The same paradox again: a writer has to go out into the world to know it, but the going out interrupts the crucial trip inwards, the making sense and shape of what you already know. This requires staying at home and being quiet.

And only when I was at my quiet task did I feel purposeful and calm, the kind of calm that circles through the blood like an added elixir, when we are doing what we are meant to be doing, and doing it gratefully.

This book—my passing mood placed under a magnifying lens—is a postscript to that very different one. A purging of the mood, and a valediction. Already I begin to feel the restlessness that longs for change, movement, novelty. Where to?

notes

p. 7   Albert Camus, *Notebooks*, 1935–42, tr. Philip Thody, Knopf, 1963, pp. 13–14

p. 8   Sinclair Lewis, *Dodsworth*, Random House Modern Library, 1947, p. 217

p. 8   W. G. Sebald, *The Emigrants*, New Directions, 1996, p. 169

p. 13   Alan Riding, "Globe-Trotting Englishwomen Who Helped Map the World," *The New York Times*, August 18, 2004

p. 14   Quoted in Iain Lundy, "In the Footsteps of Isabella Bird," *Scotsman.com*, November 8, 2005

p. 21   Yoko Tawada, *Where Europe Begins*, New Directions, 2002, p. 107

p. 29   This and all further quotes (unless indicated otherwise) are from the *Tao te Ching* in the Stephen Mitchell translation, Harper & Row, 1998

p. 30   Hilary Spurling, *Matisse the Master*, Knopf, 2005, p. 254

p. 35   Arthur Waley, *The Way and Its Power: A Study of the Tao te Ching and Its Place in Chinese Thought*, Grove Weidenfeld, 1958, p. 92

p. 37   Italo Calvino, *Invisible Cities*, Picador, 1979, p. 25

p. 40   I was reminded of Huysman's *A Rebours* and introduced to Joseph de Maistre's *Journey Around My Bedroom* by Alain de Botton's *The Art of Travel*, Pantheon, 2002

p. 41   Calvino, *Invisible Cities*, p. 108

p. 53   Allen Shawn, *Wish I Could Be There*, Viking Penguin, 2007, p. 247

p. 61   Calvino, *Invisible Cities*, p. 82

p. 63   Frigyes Karinthy, *A Journey Around My Skull*, Faber & Faber, London, 1939, translated from the Hungarian by Vernon Duckworth Barker, p. 122. Reissued in paperback in 2008 by New York Review Books.

p. 64   Karinthy, *A Journey Around My Skull*, pp.196–97

p. 65   David Dobbs, "A Depression Switch?," *The New York Times Magazine*, April 2, 2006, p. 53

p. 69   Spurling, *Matisse the Master*, p. 431

p. 74   Harry Collis, *101 American Customs*, Passport Books, 2000, p. 62

p. 97   George Eliot, *Middlemarch*, Barnes & Noble Classics, 2003, p. 183

p. 104   Quoted in Hilary Spurling, *The Unknown Matisse*, Knopf, 1998, p. 393

p. 104   Spurling, *Matisse the Master*, p. 129

p. 105   Spurling, *Matisse the Master*, p. 306 ("so dry, so crystalline"); p. 310 ("like plunging your eye . . .")

p. 111   Cyril Connolly, "England Not My England," *The Selected Essays of Cyril Connolly*, Persea, 1984, p. 84

p. 112   George Monbiot, "Flying Into Trouble," *The Nation*, May 7, 2007, pp. 33–34

p. 114   Quoted in Orvar Lofgren, *On Holiday: A History of Vacationing*, University of California Press, 1999, p. 14

p. 114-115   Lofgren, *On Holiday*, pp. 24–25

p. 116   Matt Richtel, "It Don't Mean a Thing if You Ain't Got That Ping," *The New York Times*, April 22, 2007

p. 119-121   Lofgren, *On Holiday,* pp. 231–32

p. 127   Collis, *101 American Customs*, p. 40

p. 144   Lewis, *Dodsworth*, p. 216

p. 146   Calvino, *Invisible Cities*, p. 10

p. 149   Quoted in Jenny Diski, "Excessive Bitters," *The London Review of Books*, September 7, 2006, p. 23

p. 149   Sebald, *The Emigrants*, p. 78

p. 150   Tawada, *Where Europe Begins*, p. 87

p. 155   Jonathan Freedland, "The Enigma of Ariel Sharon," *The New York Review of Books*, December 12, 2006

p. 157   Giacomo Debenedetti, *16 Ottobre 1943*, Einaudi, 2001, p. v

p. 158   Debenedetti, pp. 5–6

p. 158   Debenedetti, p. 44

p. 158   Ian Fisher, "Renewal, in Real Estate and in Culture, for Ancient People," *The New York Times*, January 26, 2007

p. 159   Debenedetti, p. vii

Printed in the United States
by Baker & Taylor Publisher Services